A Reader in Political Theology

A Reader in
Political Theology

Edited by Alistair Kee

SCM PRESS LTD

No attempt has been made to make the extracts
in this book typographically consistent. In all cases,
the spelling and punctuation etc. of the original
publisher have been used.

334 01424 7

First published 1974
by SCM Press Ltd
56 Bloomsbury Street London

© *SCM Press Ltd 1974*

Printed in Great Britain by
Northumberland Press Limited
Gateshead

To Anne

Contents

Preface

Christianity begins with a man on his way to the cross. The cross was not an altar for divine sacrifice, but the prescribed instrument by which the Romans tortured to death those who would not submit to them and who encouraged men to put their ultimate loyalties elsewhere. If Christianity is about incarnation the question is not whether political theology is still theology, but whether anything that is *without* political significance deserves the name 'theology'.

Much that is done within the area designated as theology has no political significance at all. But then it could equally well be done within the fields of archaeology, anthropology, history of classical cultures, sociology of institutions, metaphysics. These are important areas of study, but they do not claim to be about an issue which will turn *this* world upside down. They do not claim to be dealing with a new order in which the first will be last and the last first. If theology is not dealing directly with the revelation that the weakness of God is stronger than the power of corporations and alliances, that the foolishness of God is wiser than think tanks and computerized forward planning, then how can it be Christian theology? And should this not now be the criterion of theology?

Although the phrase 'political theology' has only appeared in the last few years, there has always been an interaction of theology and politics. Whole areas of the Old Testament are given over to theological reflection on the political life of Israel, critical evaluation of the nation's relationships with other powers, prophetic words in turn of judgment and promise concerning the political future of the people. If the New Testament opens with Jesus on his way to the cross it closes with his followers hounded by a political regime described as bestial. Even the silence of the New Testament on such issues as military service and slavery has its own political significance. The history of the church has been no less bound up with political life. The problem is not to find illustrations, but to stop short of a complete history of theology: Augustine on *The*

City of God, Bernard of Clairvaux on the crusades, the comity arrangement of *cuius regio eius religio*, the founding of Philadelphia, F. D. Maurice on Christian Socialism, the papal concordat with fascism, the Dutch Reformed Church of South Africa on apartheid, the World Council of Churches' 'Programme to Combat Racism'.

Theologians throughout the history of the church have addressed themselves to the political issues of the day. Sometimes the result has been to legitimize what the powerful are intent on doing anyway, to justify what the wise in any case prescribe. But even if this has happened more often than not, it would be wrong to ignore the other examples in which theologians have taken a more prophetic stand, whether in refusing to bless tyranny or in exposing the false images which capture the minds and souls of men. Theologians who address themselves to the issues which determine people's lives take a great risk. But this is the area in which faith is tested and our understanding of faith extended. Those who return to the security of the past or take off for speculative realms may never take such risks, but in what way does their work extend the faith?

Even today we are often told that religion should be kept out of politics. When this is said by politicians who refer to the blatantly political intervention of the church at various times into the political arena, then we must admit the abuses of the past. But when it is said by theologians themselves, we must simply note that it is rather late in the day for such a separation since the interaction has gone on constantly for 2,000 years. The question is not whether but what kind of interaction is to take place. The phrase 'political theology' does not indicate a completely new departure for theology: it refers to a specific relationship of politics and theology. The chapters in this book trace the development of a kind of theology from its beginnings in the Marxist-Christian dialogue through various stages to the present day. The development is set out chronologically but in the introduction to each section it can be seen that there is a process of refinement and evolution from one stage to the next. We are dealing with a new type and perspective on theology which has emerged during the last ten or fifteen years.

If theology has been mainly concerned with the past, increasingly it has been concerned with its own past. Theology can all too easily become a closed discipline which reflects on its own historical sources according to its own rules, revising its own formulations. No one outside the charmed circle has anything to contribute:

eventually no one inside the circle has anything to contribute to those outside. And if, slight complication, we have Catholic, Orthodox and Reformed circles, then at best we have emissaries attempting to communicate between circles. Such was the characteristic of ecumenical theology. Political theology, however, is to be distinguished from such a pattern in various ways. In the first place, political theology does not write its own agenda. The issues of development or violence have become central in the modern world without reference to the church. Nor does the church control the way in which these issues are debated or acted upon. Political theology sees an attempt by Christian theologians to address themselves to issues of world significance and great practical importance for all of us. But secondly, in addressing themselves to these issues theologians found themselves in mixed company, for the issues are of common concern to all traditions. What began as informal co-operation has led in time to authorized joint projects, such as the project involving the Vatican and the World Council of Churches on development, justice and peace. Political theology has therefore become doubly ecumenical, since it reflects the concern of all the churches with the whole inhabited world.

But the most obvious characteristic of political theology is that it is biased. For most of its history theology has been biased towards the political right: nor was this challenged. Political theology is biased towards the left: why should that be challenged? But there is more to it than a simple choosing of political allegiance. In the gospels Jesus is biased towards the left: he takes his place with those who are certainly not the king's men. He associates with the poor and despised rather than with the rich and influential. When challenged about this he justifies himself in parables. He takes sides apparently because God has taken sides: and to the Magnificat he adds the Beatitudes. God is biased in favour of the poor and the meek: the rich and the powerful – no matter what the church has taught – have no part in God's Kingdom. Political theology is biased because Jesus was biased.

This has not been an easy or automatic transition for theology, from the role of baptizer of the world as it is, to prophet of the world as it will be. It has involved the politicizing of theology. Theologians have become aware of the way in which theology has up till now been used to justify how things are and how they always will be. Political theology begins with the raising of consciousness among theologians to the longstanding abuse and misuse of theology. Only when this is seen is it possible to ask about the contribution of theology to the political issues of the day. Another aspect of this politicizing has been that Christian theologians have come to recognize that many themes of the political left are secularized biblical themes, themes long forgotten in the church – perhaps precisely because of their political significance. Thus Moltmann can describe Ernst Bloch as a 'Marxist with a Bible in his hand'. (It was originally intended that a section from *Das Prinzip Hoffnung* would be included in this collection, but unfortunately until there is an authorized translation of the whole work Bloch would not allow an extract to be used.)

Anyone who has followed the development of political theology, or who has participated in the movement, must feel a certain frustration that although the issues are arguably the most important ones facing the world today, it is not always clear that theology has anything to contribute. There will be no theology of revolution until there is a revolution in theology. Quite so, but very often the net result of the politicizing of theology has been that theology can no longer be used to justify the *status quo*. Perhaps this neutralizing of theology might be regarded as a sufficient gain, but there is no denying the danger that instead of going on to make an independent contribution to the issues, political theology can easily fall into the role of justifying the actions of the political left. It can uncritically take over the rhetoric of the leaders of the left, many of whom are neither poor nor meek. Political theology has begun with a radical analysis of the issues, often borrowed directly from the left. In so far as this has actually led beyond interpretation to action, the action has been joint action with the left. But there are two models of joint action. The first model characterizes Europe, and to some extent North America where Christians have participated in movements initiated and controlled by the left. They have felt the frustration of trying to see what their specific contribution might be. The second model is characteristic of Latin America where Christians have made their contribution from the outset : they have not come late to someone else's movement. Each of these models is instructive. Concerning Europe and North America, we have now entered a period in which the political left is both bankrupt of analysis and exhausted of action. There is no hope in that direction and many of its leaders know this to be so. For this reason there is a final section included on Christian Resistance. Now that there is no movement which Christians might join, no analysis to accept, no action to take, politicized Christians might well consider whether or not there are resources within their own tradition, Bible, contemplation and eucharist, which taken together would not be more politically significant than the purely political movement which has just collapsed. Moltmann's description of Bloch goes on: 'He is a Marxist with a Bible in his hand, who hoped for greater things than socialism was able to give.' When we turn to the other model, concerning Latin America, we see some of the most exciting and creative theology today deriving from the liberation movements there. But good theology does not spring from the minds of clever theologians. It is reflection on the experience and witness of authentic Christian communities. Such communities bear the marks of Christ, incarnate the truth of both Magnificat and Beatitudes, take up the cross and experience the resurrection.

There is an important lesson in this, for the state of European and American theology has not come about by chance. It has lost its way and is either arid or effete, either purely historical or dramatically supernaturalist. In *The Devil's Advocate* Cardinal Marotta observes of ecclesiastical administrators: 'We have lost touch with the people who keep us in touch with God.' The state of theology is directly linked to the fact that it is now a closed subject which does not constantly derive its material from authentic Christian communities. And more particularly we must also conclude that the life style of the theologian is of particular relevance. If theology is about knowledge that is independent of how we live our lives, either in the conceiving or the receiving of it, then it is a new gnosticism come as ever to undermine the worldliness of Christianity. But if Christian faith is about incarnation, then it is hardly surprising that Jesus left his comfortable and secure middle-class life and thriving little carpenter's business in Nazareth. He associated with the poor and despised, not to compensate them for their lot in life but because they could hear what the wise and secure could not hear. His future belongs to them.

Iona
June 1974

1 · The Christian-Marxist Dialogue

It occasionally happens that an original and creative thinker is misunderstood and underestimated in his own lifetime, to be rediscovered at a future period. In some sense what he said *becomes* true, or is now seen to apply. This could be said of Kierkegaard, whose work sank without trace in Denmark in the 1840s but was suddenly to become the basis of new developments in philosophy and theology seventy years later in Germany. At first sight the same could hardly be said of his younger contemporary, Karl Marx. Marx was a well-known Hegelian philosopher who looked to be set fair for an academic career. In the 1840s he turned to journalism and then to radical politics. He was well enough known to the governments of Germany, France and Belgium to be deported from each as a danger to public order. Yet in a sense Marx has only recently been discovered, at least in the full breadth of his thought. Until the end of World War II he was little read outside Eastern Europe and was associated with communism, economics and atheism.

By the same self-defining process as 'Socialism is what the Labour Party does', Marxism was identified in many minds with what went on in the Soviet Union. It was assumed that life in the USSR represented the outworking of Marx's teaching and also that Marx's interests went no further than the public utterances of the leaders of that country. Even many of those in the West who were sympathetic to the aims of the October Revolution were disillusioned with developments under Stalin. 'Communism' became a pejorative word in the West and Marxism was simply the ideological basis for an inhuman and often bestial form of government. Although Marx originally published his works in Germany his writings have been made available in this century through the Moscow edition. Not surprisingly, attention was concentrated on his later economic writings. This has been unfortunate for his reputation, since by modern definition he was not a particularly good economist. But at least in the tradition of Adam Smith and David Ricardo, Marx knew very well that economics are always in practice political economy. His economic writings reflect his political and social concerns which in turn stem from his early humanist (not forgetting his Jewish prophetic) judgments on inequality and injustice. But of these concerns, little was known in the West between the wars.

Finally, the name of Marx was associated with strident atheism. It was almost as if he had invented it. In the course of the Enlightenment and the Romantic movement in Germany there was a style of free-thinking which did not even bother to oppose religion. It was regarded as an embarrassing and unworthy stage in the ascent of man. Marx was distinguished from the 'despisers of religion' by regarding it as a real and persistent force in society. It was not an insignificant survival from early times which would automatically die out. For Marx it was a very important factor in shaping human history (distorting it, as he thought) and it had to be strenuously opposed. The fact that he opposed religion for the sake of a more humane and just social order was entirely forgotten.

In so far as the West was counter-revolutionary, committed to capitalism and nominally Christian, then Marx appeared as the very epitome of all that must be opposed and resisted. There was no Marxist-Christian dialogue: there was nothing to discuss. On the contrary, in the Senate hearings of the 1950s we see not dialogue but a holy crusade against Marxism. The papacy which acted so ambiguously on Fascism had no qualms about excommunicating members of the Communist Party.

The possibility of dialogue came about with changes on both sides. On the Communist side there were the revelations by Khrushchev at the twentieth Party Congress of at least some of the atrocities of the Stalinist period. This, taken together with the revulsion among many Communists outside the USSR at the invasion of Hungary, enabled a very important practical distinction to emerge between Stalinism and Marxism, between what happened in the Soviet Union and what Marxists stood for. 1957 saw the emergence of the 'New Left' comprising ex-Communists and non-Communists. The availability of the early writings of Marx at this time led to a very positive and far-reaching revising of the nature and goals of Marxism. On the question of religion, neo-Marxism is less inclined to make atheism an issue and is more likely to challenge Christians to be true to the original revolutionary elements of primitive Christianity.

On the Christian side the most important influence came from J. L. Hromadka of the Comenius Faculty of Theology in Prague. In the spirit of Jan Comenius, the seventeenth-century theologian who had actually proposed an international court of peace and a plan for general disarmament, Hromadka organized the Christian Peace Conference, in 1958. The All-Christian Peace Assemblies followed, in 1961, 1964 and finally 1968, and brought together Christians not only on an ecumenical basis but from East and West and eventually from the Third World.

One of the earliest examples of Christian interest in Marxism was the Marxism Commission of the Study Fellowship of the Evangelical Academies in Germany during 1958-59, but perhaps the most significant meeting during which both sides were well represented took place in Czechoslovakia in 1967. This was the joint meeting at Mariánské Lázně sponsored by the Paulus-Gesellschaft and the Sociological Institute of the Czechoslovakian Academy of Sciences. This was witness to the steady change in the attitude of the Roman Catholic Church during this period. The change may be traced from the accession of Pope John XXIII in 1958. René Laurentin sees here a transition from a tendency to criticize and condemn the world to a more universal openness to the world and an expectation of goodness in men. The climate for dialogue was more favourable with the publication of *Mater et Magistra* (1961) and *Pacem in Terris* (1963). Through the ecumenical work of Hromadka and others the World Council of Churches was actively involved in the dialogue, for example the 1968 Consultation of Christians and Marxists in Geneva.

The dialogue has been carried on at the level of world conferences but also more informally within countries and in local communities. The progress has been dependent very often on particular circumstances. Thus in France the memory of co-operation in the wartime resistance movement has meant that the dialogue has been carried on from a basis of some trust. Roger Garaudy is the best-known contributor to this dialogue. His expulsion from the Central Committee of the Communist Party further emphasizes present confusion among Communists after the invasion of Czechoslovakia. Santiago Carrillo, as General Secretary of the Communist Party of Spain, maintained that denying the existence of God is not a priority among Communists. He has spoken warmly of the statements by J. M. Gonzales-Ruis on human autonomy and creativity. In Italy Luigi Longo has repeated the call of Palmiro Togliatti at the Tenth Party Congress for dialogue with the church. In Britain the most interesting example of the dialogue has been the Slant group of Catholic Marxists in the late 1960s.

With this reference to Slant we can end this introduction with a few qualifications to the idea of 'dialogue'. In some cases the dialogue is localized in the extreme, for it means the on-going search of those who are themselves committed both to Marxism and to Christianity. *How* this can be so is not yet clear: *that* it is so is a fact of our time. Secondly, 'dialogue' to some extent misrepresents the present contact between Marxists and Christians. It gives the impression that they are primarily concerned with a theoretical exchange of views, an exploration of different systems of belief. More often the contact takes place on the basis of common concerns and joint action, as competing interpretations of the world give way to a common attempt to change it. Finally, although anyone who has a faith will want others to share it, the contact of Marxists and Christians is not characterized by attempts to proselytize. More often the Marxists are challenged to examine their own dogmas which come from Stalinism or old guard Communism and which bring about false consciousness. The Christians may well be challenged to free themselves from cultural Constantinianism, to distinguish Christian judgments from middle-class assumptions. Both sides have not only rediscovered elements lost sight of in their own traditions; they have found their own positions developed and enriched, without necessarily any weakening of conviction.

Jan Milic Lochman · *Christian-Marxist Dialogue*

Jan Milic Lochman, *Church in a Marxist Society*, SCM Press, London and Harper & Row, NY 1970, pp.174-77, 189

In recent times from both sides has emerged the concept of *humanization* to characterize this shared concern of Christians and Marxists. This is certainly justified; humanizing social conditions is clearly our common concern. Still this concept is very general. If we are not able to fill this general idea with a more concrete content, the concept of convergence will be too narrow. Indeed, when we consider the exact meaning of humanization, especially when dealing with the question of what belongs to the 'dimensions of the humane,' the consensus between Marxism and the Christian message is much broader.

If I were to express this convergence in a very fragmentary and abbreviated way, using three major topics, I would select the concepts of society, history, and the future. The Marxist and Christian view of man emphatically states, to start with, that *man is a social creature*. Man is not an abstract, isolated creature content in himself. He lives in association with others. He is a social being. That is the fundamental qualification of his existence, and that is the delimitation of his being as a man. He has to be in an actual solidarity with other men, not bound up in concern for his own individuality only. That is the way of human fulfillment in a personal and social sense. Above all, that solidarity means fellowship with the poor and oppressed, the weary and heavy-laden – including the concern for a more just society. This stance of solidarity, this 'socialistic impulse,' distinguishes Christianity and Marxism from other orientations that place more emphasis on individual possibilities.

There is another shared attitude: *We both take history seriously* as a significant dimension of human existence. Man is not an abstract, general, metaphysically prefabricated substance. He is a historical creature. By that I do not mean that he is an abstract individual, possessing 'historicity,' but rather that he exists and participates within the concretely given historical conditions and relations. Living in this historical context, he is no mere object in history; he is also history's subject and agent. History is his sphere of responsibility. History is the forum in which his business is transacted.

In this connection we come to the third shared concept: Christian and Marxist thought is *thinking directed to the future*. Man is *homo viator*, man on the way. He is on his way to a future destination. He is not tied down to a once-for-all-time given status quo. On the contrary, his heart belongs to that which will come. What is at hand is not enough for him. He must think about the promises of a greater justice. And in the light of that greater justice, he must not only interpret but change his world.

None of these converging motifs shared by Christians and Marxists can be simply stated without some qualification. None of these motifs excludes rather divergent aspects of these conceptions. What Marxism and the Christian message have in common under the topics of society, history, and the future is not identical. Therefore, when we think of the dialogue between the two, we must always consider the serious tensions between them.

Nevertheless, what I have indicated about the convergence between them is not an illusion. Their concentration upon these dimensions of man's existence clearly differentiates them from many other possible philosophical, religious, and political analyses of man, for example, the existentialist and the positivistic perspectives. Such a concentration makes them closely related partners of an authentic dialogue and social cooperation.

There is, as already indicated, a serious *difference* between Marxism and the Christian message. If I were to define more closely the decisive difference, I would cite the *question of God*. I recognize that precisely this difference can be viewed as an outmoded and consequently superseded recognition. Does the question of God really draw a genuine boundary line between Marxism and the Christian message? Hasn't theology today become quite cautious and hesitant exactly in this respect? Does the concept of God really belong to the 'essence of Christian faith'? Many theologians today ask these questions.

From the other side, paradoxically, this question seems to be less fixed than ever. The saying that 'God is not entirely dead' is heard from Marxist quarters, and from conversations with them we learn that the concern for transcendence is taken quite seriously by many present-day Marxists. Does the fundamental difference really rest on this point?

If I answer this question affirmatively, then I must hasten to add that in the 'question of God' I do not refer to a metaphysical concept of God that we must establish as an absolute boundary over against the historical, dynamic, and social orientation of Marxist thought. Such a metaphysical concept would be a completely false boundary. The God of whom I am speaking is not the God of the philosophers, but the God of Abraham, Isaac, and Jacob.

Consequently, God is not the God of a metaphysical scheme but the God of history, of society, of the future – all in the concrete sense of the gospel of God's way for mankind in Jesus Christ. That is a transcendence that does not alienate man, one that does not divest man of his historical and social dimension, one that *does* free him for history, for social life, for the future. Furthermore, this transcendence is what sets the situation of man in a new light – the light of grace.

That is what I mean by the question of God : *the transcendence of grace*. Marxism disavows the question of God, seeing in it an improper turning away from man's concrete and worldly obligations. In view of the misuse of religion in the course of history, Marxism has solid grounds for its atheism. Dedication to the great task of the revolutionary refashioning of this world must not be

watered down with 'pious reasons.' Christians should fully understand that, too. The gospel treats the world in utter seriousness.
At the centre of the gospel stands the proclamation of the *incarnation* of God. But exactly and specifically, it is the incarnation of
God. If God is ideologically denied, man is threatened to become
dissolved in his history, his society, and his future, and he becomes
imprisoned in his immanence and his worldly projects. The
penultimate becomes the ultimate for him. His total destiny then
depends on his accomplishments. He lives with the possibilities of
happiness and euphoria as they emerge in moments of his successes.
But he also lives in frustration and despair as they are given in the
situation of defeat and guilt.

Over against all of this the Christian message speaks of the
transcendence of grace as the ultimate dimension of human existence. The *transcendence*: man is never used up completely in his
social and historical conditions. His future is greater than the
future of his accomplishments. He is more than he is. And the
Christian message speaks of *grace*: our salvation is not related to
our efficiency or the failure of our attempts. Our accomplishment
is not what is ultimate. The ultimate is not our sin – so, too, it
is not death for us. The ultimate, the proper future of man, is
grace.

The real task of Christians in their encounter with Marxists
appears to me to be to testify to this condition of being human.
The church's mission lies exactly in this witness – in all societies,
especially in a Marxist society. This is her authentic difference
from the society; it is a difference that does not set her at a distance
from others but one that unites her with them in Christian solidarity,
a practical proof of the transcendence of grace. If the church
fashions and promulgates laws instead of this message, she understands herself as an ideological anti-power set against Marxism
(and how often she has done so!). If she does that, she misses her
unique and most distinctive contribution and witness for society;
she becomes worthless salt.

In his lecture before the symposium [at Mariánské Lázně], Milan
Prucha made a remarkable attempt to develop a new Marxist
approach to the problem of man. He did so on the background of
the classical philosophical approach to the problem of being. Prucha
clearly refused to reduce the anthropological problem to the
historical and social dimensions of man. It is true that man is a
historical and a social being, but these important dimensions of
human life do not represent the full range of humanity. In this

connection, the question of real transcendence was posed. Prucha answered it by a reference to the concept of being, which must not be fixed prematurely either through the concept of matter (as in the case of traditional materialism) or through the concept of God (as is the case in religious tradition). In this connection Prucha undertook a criticism of theology from an unexpected angle. He confessed that, in the course of the Marxist-Christian dialogue, 'our Christian friends have awakened in us the courage and appetite for transcendence.' But the question must be referred back to them and radicalized. Christians do not manage to keep the problem of transcendence in its true profoundness but tend to link transcendence with 'particularity.' This is evident from the fact that they immediately 'define' transcendence by the concept 'God.'

A philosopher must avoid this step. Face to face with this theological temptation, Marxism has a chance for interpellation of a different type than in the past. In the future, it might be its task not so to apply the brake on the Christian hankering after transcendence but, on the contrary, to free it from its religious trammels.

Giulio Girardi · *Christian Humanism Face to Face with Marxism*

Giulio Girardi, *Marxism and Christianity*, Gill & Son, Dublin and Macmillan Co., NY 1968, pp.130-37. Reprinted by permission. © 1968 by M. H. Gill & Son Ltd

As we have been noting from the beginning, the problem of convergences and divergences between Marxism and Christianity cannot be broken down into a multitude of details. It bears primarily on central inspirations. At this level it would be difficult to exaggerate the profundity of the divergences separating the two systems, for they are present everywhere, and since we are dealing with basically unified systems, these divergences confer differences of meaning on every expression of life and thought. For the same reason, however, neither can the profundity of the convergences be denied. They, too, are present everywhere and ensure that differences in meaning are never total. This dual aspect of the relationship seems to explain the contrasting attitudes taken up in the Christian world towards Marxism, ranging from indiscriminate rejection to facile concordism. The divergences are concealed in formulae very Christian in appearance, while the convergences are expressed in formulae markedly anti-Christian in appearances. Hence the difficulty of drawing an objective demarcation line between convergences and divergences. They are co-present every-where. Hence, too, the particular complexity of dialogue with Marxism.

Difficulty is not impossibility, however. If our interpretation is valid, the convergences, however delicate the task of pin-pointing them may be, exist and are profound. They can form the basis of fruitful doctrinal dialogue (I do not intend to raise here the question of dialogue in the sense of political collaboration. This raises quite different problems and in any case lies outside my competence).

A central aspect of this dialogue might well be the question of humanism, which separates convergences from divergences fairly clearly. In the crisis of truth and of values that marks our times, both Marxism and Christianity claim to be unified and complete world-views, capable of giving meaning to a host of details in the light of the totality, of transforming everyday life with the sparkle of idealism, and of bringing a message of hope to man. It is a question, not just of doctrinal systems, but of types of personality and civilization. These visions aim to enable man to fulfil himself as an end. They direct his action and the movement of history and of nature to this end. They support an ethic in which the absolute value of man is a fundamental principle and the com-mandment of love occupies a central position. In the pursuit of this ideal, man is not just an instrument; he is the principal architect through personal and communal action. His action is aimed at the construction of an earthly city in which men will be able to live together and in which man will really be an end. In particular, this implies the humanization of the economic relationship. This relationship conditions man's total development and is responsible for the fact that his influence on history is exercised largely through his influence on the economic infrastructures. The humanist ideal and its realization are essentially social matters. Man will fulfil himself only in a community, and his action towards this end will be effective only when communal. The horizons of this community are not circumscribed by any particular region or category, but stretch to the ends of the earth. The communal character of the human vocation is especially evident in the social function of wealth and in the legalization of state intervention to limit private property when it appears to conflict with its social function. Social action to realize these objectives sets off from a situation of alienation that can be overcome only by doing battle with those who attempt to canonize it. This war is waged within existing structures but tends to reform them; in this sense it can become revolutionary. The world-view that inspires action cannot control it effectively unless it has been critically justified itself, and is capable of accepting the contributions of science. Therefore, it must recognize the fundamental reality of matter, particularly matter as constitutive of man, his causality and the laws of his being. The whole of history is constituted by a vast movement to liberate and unify man, the human community and the whole universe.

It is difficult to contest the fact that convergence is real and profound on these points, not to mention others. Along with this we should place the critique of the many alienations defined in contrast with these values. With regard to religious alienation in particular, the Christian is in agreement with the Marxist precisely insofar as religion actually alienates.

If this is true, then we must admit that some of Christianity's most characteristic intuitions recoil against it. How is this fact to be explained? History has undoubtedly occasional versions of Christianity in which these intuitions were lost sight of on the practical, and even on the theoretical, plane. Thus Christianity has been criticized in the name of Christian values and compromised in syntheses that are not Christian. But perhaps it is an over-simplification of the problem to say that Christianity has merely 'lost sight of' some of its truths, that these have been rediscovered by other systems, and all that Christianity has to do is recover what it once possessed by returning to the spirit of its origins.

In reality, many of these 'Christian' truths are present only virtually in primitive Christianity and in the inspired books themselves. In other words, we find the principles from which these truths may be inferred, but not the truths themselves. It would be difficult to show, for example, that the social encyclicals of recent popes are derived purely from revelation. More generally, it would be inexact to affirm that all the spiritual problems of our time are resolved in the Gospels, even if the Gospels supply the inspiration and the broad directives which make their solutions possible, as well as the germs from which these solutions mature. One must acknowledge a certain incompleteness in revelation with regard to new situations and new problems. The Christian community, under the direction of the *magisterium*, has a duty, in this area too, to supply 'what is wanting' in divine intervention, or more precisely, to lay itself open to divine action, which continues to animate history. The fidelity of Christianity to its origins cannot be simply conservative but also must be creative. Christians have been guilty, not only of losing sight of ancient truths, but also of failing to discover new ones when they were needed in new situations; not only of failing to put doctrine into practice, but also of neglecting to develop doctrine itself in keeping with the rhythm of history.

It follows that in affirming the evangelical inspiration of certain truths present in other systems, e.g., in Marxism, Christianity does not intend to question the originality of what these systems contribute to the evolution of human knowledge or to claim all the historical credit for itself.

In fact it cannot be denied that this evolution of mankind stimulates the evolution of Christianity itself and that, consequently, movements like Marxism, which arose in opposition to religion, may subsequently contribute to its maturation and enrichment. By focusing attention anew on the basis of the problem, this process can help, in turn, to reveal the need, e.g., in Marxism, for re-thinking and maturation.

Awareness of the convergences and of the basis which they provide for dialogue obviously cannot lead to any camouflaging of the divergences, even to serve the needs of dialogue itself. They spring up just as soon as any of the points enumerated above are dealt with in greater detail. The most macroscopic of them derives, as I mentioned earlier, from atheism. In order to measure its profundity we shall have to attempt a more direct reply to the question of whether Marxism is essentially atheistic.

First, let it be noted that the term 'essential', as applied to a doctrinal system, is not always very clear. We need to distinguish at least three meanings of the term:

(a) In the strict sense, doctrines that regulate all the others, or at least the most original tenets, are essential to a system – for these we shall reserve the qualification 'fundamental'.

(b) Essential in a broader sense are doctrines whose role is to give global significance to the world-view. They may be fundamental or derivative.

(c) Other doctrines necessarily connected with those already mentioned may be termed essential in an even broader sense.

The importance of these distinctions, which may appear rather academic, will emerge more clearly when we apply them to Marxism.

First of all, if our interpretation is correct, it seems reasonably clear that in sense 'c', atheism is essential to Marxism. In other words, it is not a purely personal tenet of Marx, but a thesis connected with the foundations of his system.

Again in sense 'b', atheism seems to be essential to Marxism. It does not merely affect certain sectors of the system; it traverses all its solutions and characterizes Marxist humanism as a whole. We have seen at every stage of the exposition how the various tenets of Marxism invoke atheism.

Finally, with regard to sense 'a', we must be much more cautious. As a denial, atheism (in Marxism as in other systems) is a derived, not a primitive, position. Therefore, the assertions that demand it are independent of it. In other words, atheism is not one of the 'fundamental' theses of Marxism.

So it is that the affirmation of the absolute value of man, along with many of its implications in the fields of ontology, morals, economics, theory of knowledge, etc., does not demand atheism. I have attempted to prove, on the contrary, that these theories can be actuated in many cases only on the hypothesis that God exists. If they lead to atheism, this is because they are joined to another decisive principle, that of the existence of axiological rivalry between man and God, human action and divine action, human reality and divine reality, and, consequently, between morality and religion, secular (especially economic) values and sacred values, the community spirit and the religious spirit, etc. This principle is not itself atheistic and is often developed, as we have seen, in deeply religious contexts. This means that Marxist atheism derives from two ranges of premises, neither of which, taken separately, demands it. Each is in fact susceptible to development in a religious direction.

Insofar as the political, economic, social theories, etc., of Marxism are dissociated from the principle of axiological rivalry, they no longer imply atheism either as a presupposition or as a consequence. By acknowledging the existence of a revolutionary side to religion, the Marxists already seem to have done some re-thinking on this principle.

It remains true, nevertheless, that to dissociate the political, economic and social theories of Marxism from the principle of axiological rivalry is not the same as to affirm their compatibility with Christianity. Christianity, as we saw earlier, is not just an answer to the problem of God. It is also an answer to the problem of man. Its resources in the face of Marxism are deployed from these two points of view. They call Marxist humanism itself into question. In other words, serious antinomies subsist within the Marxist system and within the concept of *praxis*, so that the humanistic inspiration is constantly grappling with anti-humanistic elements.

Any doctrinal or practical thesis that contradicts the absolute value of man may be termed anti-humanistic. Opposition to humanism could come either from the prospect of a world in which not every man would have the opportunity of fulfilling himself as an end, or from the prospect of a system of values that would not guarantee the respect of men for each other. Now, as we have seen, a life in which death had the last word could not be considered fulfilled, could not be considered to have realized its fundamental aspirations. A love that ended in death, a community destined to disintegrate, a history in which, in order to build up mankind, one had to lose oneself – these things do not constitute victory over alienation. A system of values made radically dependent on history and on the party does not guarantee respect for man, nor, in consequence, the possibility of life in fraternal community. Such dependence would mean that, structurally, alienation could never be overcome. And if the criterion of value coincides with the success of a particular institution, e.g., the party, then the movement is exposed to the constant temptation to impose itself on the masses and re-establish the enslavement of the majority by a minority.

The basic problem posed by the re-thinking of Marxism seems to be reducible to the question of whether *praxis* is the sole criterion of value. This leads back, in turn, to the fundamentally socio-economic and partitic vision of the ideal. Hence the historicization of values (particularly moral values) and truth; the monolithic inclination in axiology and the denial of autonomy to the various areas of secular and religious values; the idea that the party dictates what is valuable and what is true (leading to the pre-eminence of the institution over the person and the community, and of the 'objective' over the 'subjective').

What the Christian will reproach the Marxist for, in the last analysis, is not the fact that he is a humanist, but that he is not humanist enough; nor the fact that he does battle with alienation, but that he does not do so radically enough; nor again the fact that he denounces the master-slave dialectic, but that he remains a victim in his turn.

What he must do is not to import values in an eclectic way, but to get back to the roots of his original personalistic and communal inspiration, to insert socio-economic *praxis* more decisively into the whole scheme of things, and thus to arrive, by way of maturation from within, at a pluralistic expression of the criterion of value and of faith. In a word, Marxism must become decidedly more faithful to man.

Helmut Gollwitzer · *Messianism and Atheism*

Helmut Gollwitzer, *The Christian Faith and the Marxist Criticism of Religion*, The Saint Andrew Press, Edinburgh and Charles Scribner's Sons, NY 1970, pp.81-82, 89-92, 95-98, 101-103. Reprinted by permission. © The Saint Andrew Press 1970

Our previous discussion has described the type of criticism of religion which has prevailed in Marxist Communism up to the present day. No new elements have been introduced, only the changing historical situation and the tactical needs of the moment have caused changes of emphasis. In Leninism a more relaxed attitude of disregard has been replaced by 'militant atheism', the commitment of the party to anti-religious agitation – as Leninism in general is Marxism in a hurry – a fact which can in part be explained by the extraneous elements of Russian revolutionary thinking which have poured into it, and in part by the secret anxiety lest the European proletariat should fail to achieve its task for humanity, and history accordingly not take the course prescribed for it by Marx. With the voluntaristic trait in Leninism, atheism also becomes militant.

But the hardening of the socialistic movement in an anti-religious mould occurred at an earlier point. The toleration within the party of church members was never regarded by Marx and Engels (who, as above noted, insisted upon it) as relativizing the fundamental conflict between socialism and religion. But to describe the views of the two spiritual fathers is not to answer the question 'Why did the socialist movement adopt the anti-religious attitude?' It was in the nineteenth century that this chiefly happened, and it held good for the Communist part of the movement, while in the social-democratic part in the different European lands, the bond between socialism and atheism was to a greater or less degree dissolved. But why not also in the Communist movement?

Our question, which, as can be seen, it is by no means easy to answer, can in my opinion only be answered in a twofold manner by citing two co-operative elements of a quite diverse kind. The first is empirical knowledge, the second is Messianism.

By empirical knowledge I mean the actual things which a revolutionary social movement in the Europe of the nineteenth century was able and compelled to experience and observe in its encounter with the official representatives of Christianity – and by this I mean not only the ecclesiastical officials but also the circle of Church members taking part in religious life. These experiences, reinforced by a study of religious history, could be generalized in theoretic form. However, it must at once be noted that this element is little mentioned in Marxist theory. Empirical knowledge has only an illustrative function, and serves at the best as a subsequent confirmation of what was already known about the essence of religion ...

For this reason not only the Church, but religion was the object of criticism.

But in our search for the reasons why atheism was exalted into a dogma for a whole movement we must not let ourselves be deceived by this. The development in England, where from the beginning Christian allies in the fight were visibly present, is a positive proof, as the development in Russia where the unity of State and Church made the latter a prop of the existing order is a negative proof of the fundamental importance of the historical experiences of this movement in relation to the Church. Where in his wanderings could the tailor's apprentice Weitling, or the turner's apprentice Bebel, have found a manse in the Germany of that day in which a sermon would not have been preached to him on submission to his fate and humble acknowledgment of the divinely decreed order as the bearing which God required of him? From what pulpit was the collapse of the Revolution of 1848 not interpreted as a judgment of God? Where was there any sign that the Church did not identify itself with the programme of a 'Christian State' under Friedrich Wilhem IV, and did not gratefully profit from it? Was it not evident to the thoughtful member of the proletariat that the economic order under which he suffered could not be interpreted in the categories of an idealist history? In those circles of the Church which were sensitive to the desperate urgency of the social question, were people not incapable of forming an adequate theory for its diagnosis and cure? And did not therefore all social effort remain – to use a vivid comparison of Eduard Thurneysen – like a too small lid on too large a pot? Did not the urgency of material need and the object lessons taught by material work compel the proletarian to a materialistic understanding of the world, in contrast with which the idealism cherished by the Church necessarily appeared as a pale, unrealistic, misleading and deliberate confusion of the real issues? Did not theology interpret Christian faith in idealist categories, Platonic instead of Hebrew, so that it was easy to take Christianity for a special kind of idealist world-view? Walter Dirks is right: 'When the proletariat opened its eyes a hundred years ago and awakened to self-consciousness, it is not true that Christ was arrogantly rejected; it would be much truer to say that in a sense Christ was not there at all. Christ was invisible and inaudible. When the old Christian order of life for the peasantry and the people of the small towns was no longer viable for the proletarian, because he had been lifted out of this order into a completely different strange order, Christ should have been made visible to him in a new way through the mediation of "Christians" who had entered into his existence in the power of Christian sacrifice. This did not happen. No Christian of stature at that point broke through the barrier between middle-class, the peasant class, and the feudal class. And so Christ remained invisible.... Let us be pitilessly clear on this point: this is how "Marxism" came into existence. The Marxists fell into error, but the greater part of the blame lay with the Christians. The recognition of this fact must strike a deadly blow at the roots of all Christian self-satisfaction in relation to Marxism. The burden of proletarian unbelief lies on *our* shoulders. This unbelief does not separate us from these men, it actually binds us to them.'

For our inquiry we can draw hence the conclusion that, when the movement adopted the atheism of individuals as a general doctrine, its experience of the Church and its visible representatives was a decisive factor. We cannot know how things might have gone without this factor, but we can assume that the resistant power of experiences of a contrary character might have been sufficient, even in the moment of decision for the revolutionary character of the movement, to compel the drawing of a distinction between the socio-political elements and the philosophical anti-religious horizon of Marxist doctrine. But as it was, the things that men everywhere experienced at the hands of the Church, and the things that they observed in it, led straight to the adoption of this horizon, rather than refuting it.

And yet it would be wrong to see the empirical factor as the only one. It was necessary that there should be another, which involved a decision which is certainly 'irrational', without thereby being regarded as demonic. It was the decision to give Communism as 'the doctrine of the conditions of the liberation of the proletariat' such an expansion that the struggle received over and above its socio-political goal an eschatological Messianic character, or, more precisely, it was the decision to adopt the expansion which this doctrine had received at the hands of Marx and Engels. This expansion was indeed traditional among the early socialists, who also were unable to paint the necessary social revolution in any other than the eschatological colours of paradise. This meant that the labour movement was already receptive for the Marxist perspective. How far this absolute perspective should be obligatory on the movement, how far it must and should give up its right as the firstborn to its task in world-history, for the mess of pottage of particular improvements, this has in consequence been a problem causing division within the labour movement, which gave rise to the opposition between reformism and revolution, between trade-unionism and Leninism, and which is a latent factor in the conflicts between the factions of Communism today; the Messianic exaggeration begets ever again the temptation of a merely pragmatic way of thinking, and a limitation to the tasks of the day.

And with all this it is impossible to decide the question which reaches into the unfathomable depths of the human heart, whether the absolute character of the chosen goal is the result of the repudiation of religion, or on the contrary, has caused it. The rejection of faith in God may be the consequence of a defiant and triumphant emancipatory self-assertion of man. But this self-assertion can also have the function of positively filling the vacuum which came into existence through the preceding disillusionment with the Church and the disintegration of religion. Both factors may in the history of modern thought have indistinguishably influenced each other as cause and effect; the claim of God was doomed to rejection because it was understood as hindering and competing with the claim of man to self-development, which – whatever its grounds may have been – was asserting itself with great force. On the other hand man needed a new prospect of earthly self-development as a substitute and consolation for the loss of the faith which had been destroyed by the Enlightenment, and for the loss of the rich sense of significance which is given by faith. Thus absolute Communism needs atheism, but equally atheism, in so far as it is not able to tolerate resignation, needs earthly promises of so absolute a character as those Communism provides. Thus the Marxist formulae, too, can quite well be reversed; when man loses heaven (perhaps through the discovery that it is empty) how else shall he console himself than with the earth, and in what other way than by cheating himself with the illusion that the earth is capable of producing a compensatory consolation, and that only the hitherto imperfect conditions are to blame for the fact that men had not hitherto believed that it was able to provide such consolation? The liberation of the proletariat must at the same time be the liberation of man in general, the introduction of the absolute society, in which the interests of the individual and the interests of the species, coincide, in which the riddle of history is solved, in which, as George Lukacs often wrote, it becomes evident that however tragic the fate of the individual existence may be, the lot of man as a whole is not tragic; in which man's wishes which go beyond his earthly life are a thing of the past, have 'died out' because he finds in fellowship the fulfilment of all his genuine needs. By fighting for itself, the proletariat becomes the fulcrum for the great, universal change; but for this reason it must never fight for itself alone, 'it's Fatherland must be greater'.

And so this worldly eschatology with its Messianism is the internal ground of the dogmatic affirmation of atheism, as the empirical knowledge of the Church was its external ground. The fighter in a revolution with a goal of this kind cannot get on without a revolutionary metaphysic, without a general picture of the world, without a 'world-view'. The goal, seen in the vision, seized by the will, requires a world-picture which justifies it in thought. The break-away from religion happens just at this point; Marxism becomes a sustitute-religion by becoming a substitute source of meaning. From this standpoint it is understandable how well-founded individual objections of a historical, logical, politico-economic nature often cut no ice in discussion with our Communist partners. This world-view was not in fact conceived to satisfy the theoretic questions of a mind in repose. No, it is a fighting doctrine, and therefore satisfies so long as the objective of the battle is believed in, and the loyalty of the fighting-group is intact. If reality contradicts the doctrine – then, in good Hegelian fashion – so much the worse for reality! The fighter wills that the world should be as it is here conceived, because he can then realize his goal. Or: because the world is as it is, there is therefore nowhere a goal and meaning for man except in this perspective of the attainable absolute society within history. The deepest roots of this atheism are thus – contrary to the official claims – not theoretic, not 'scientific', but practical. Atheism is the postulate; God cannot exist because his existence would exclude self-redemption. But this postulate can, as already stated, have grown from the deeper soil of the experience of meaninglessness after the disintegration and loss of faith in God; it cried out to be transcended in the discovery of a new meaning. This has happened here, and the confident tone expresses the conviction that the crisis which originated with the question about the meaning of existence without God, has been successfully surmounted. All theoretic argumentation *pro et contra* conceals the existential ground of the decisions; it can only confirm these after the event, give weapons for the fight. But the decisions are taken at a deeper level. This means, however, that the man who makes the decisions, and who is to be led beyond a previous decision, must be sought for at a deeper level than that at which he would at first like to carry on the discussion.

Atheism as the obligatory doctrine of a revolutionary movement is then once and for all bound up with the fate of an absolute eschatology of immanence. And this itself is once and for all bound up with the progress and fate of the movement and its struggle. However absolutely it may be formulated as allegedly timeless truth, it belongs all the same to the historically-conditioned ideology of the movement, conditioned by the mental, social, and political climate of the time of its origin, by the development of the relation between faith and science, by its experiences from time to time in relation to religious groups, and last but not least by the difference of the situation before and after it seizes political power, i.e. by its failure to realize its programme. The doctrine does not continue permanently unchanged through the changes of experience and situation. And here we must note that a movement, so long as it is still looking forward to the seizure of power, can turn a blinder eye in its doctrine to the influence of historical process than later; its adherence to its Utopia is less likely to be disputed. After the seizure of power it is in the saddle, the conservative tendency of possession, the desire to keep things as they are, influences it, and at the same time the responsibility for a concrete society for men, for their existence and needs, is not permanently to be ignored. Further, there is the testing-out of projects in their execution, there are the reverses, the unforeseen new factors, the differences of opinion which now begin to show even in the ranks of the rulers, the different national conditioning factors, and so on, and the eventually resulting loss of the monolithic character of the movement, which was so much easier to maintain in the days of struggle. Finally, there is the great problem, intractable to the direction of even very strong leaders, of handing over to the next generations, a problem which repeatedly causes the older generation to experience the limits of its own power and influence.

At a distance from reality goals are often formulated as absolute Utopias (so once was even the liberal Utopia, whose fruits even the conservatives of the West today would never wish to renounce!). But on a nearer prospect expectations become more sober. The attainable is separated from the unattainable. The Utopian absolute formulation had its historical function as a stimulant, but it cannot be turned into the prose of reality.

2 · Theology of Hope

The most formative influence on Marx was not Hegel but the Bible. When the writings of the young Marx became available in the West, Marxism was seen to be not only a form of humanism, but specifically Western humanism, closely linked to the biblical view of man and society. In his earliest extant essays, written at the Trier Gymnasium at the age of seventeen, Marx was already facing the problem of what a young man of ability should do with his life. Should he use his talents to further his career, or should he dedicate them to the service of others? He chose the latter, not in any romantic way, and dedicated the rest of his life to uncovering the ills of society and their root causes. What are the factors which control, distort and restrict men's lives and prevent their fulfilment? How can this situation be changed?

The new dialogue with Marxism is possible because of the recovery of the humanist concerns of the early Marx. Thus in the work of Milan Prucha and Roger Garaudy a great deal of attention is paid to the question of transcendence, not in its alienating form of supernaturalism, but in relation to the enquiry about man's potential and quest for fulfilment. Hence the aphorism of Ernst Bloch: 'What is decisive – to transcend without transcendence' (*Atheism in Christianity*).

Ernst Bloch himself should occupy a prominent position in this section. Unfortunately, however, it is not possible to allow him to speak for himself. He claims to have written his magnum opus *Das Prinzip Hoffnung* in the USA during World War II, and it was published in Germany in 1959, but it has yet to appear in English. Attempts at translation have been made, but the length of the work (over 1500 pages) and the great complexity of Bloch's style have so far proved insuperable difficulties. Bloch has refused to authorize a translation, and consequently those who do not read German can only glimpse the work through discussions in English. One such discussion, by Josef Pieper, has been included here;

apart from that it is only possible briefly to make some salient points.

There is a danger in concentrating attention on Marxists who say odd and interesting things, but who are completely unrepresentative of even the new lines of neo-Marxism. But Bloch has a special place in the development of political theology, not least because he is a Marxist non-practising Jew. So far have we come from Stalinism and strident anti-religious propaganda that Bloch claims that to call him an atheist does not describe him at all. In fact he throws out a gentle counter that as a Jew he has simply carried the second commandment one step further. Or in another aphorism: 'Only an atheist can be a good Christian; only a Christian can be a good atheist.' Before leaving this point we should recall that Bloch was not alone at that time in raising the question of hope. The Polish Marxist philosopher Leszek Kolakowski wrote his famous essay 'The Priest and the Jester: Reflections on the Theological Heritage of Contemporary Thinking' a few years before Bloch's book appeared, and there claims that the first question taken over from theology is that of eschatology.

There are two elements in Bloch's work which have particular significance for theology. The first is his concern for transcendence, the belief that man is not a finished being but is in process of moving beyond his present situation. His work is therefore given a future orientation which has proved suggestive for theology and has led to the theology of hope. The second element concerns Bloch's claim to find an underground Bible, traditions in the Bible which represent continuing criticism and unrest with the order of things. Taken together these two things mean that Christian faith is not only concerned vitally with the future – indeed must be characterized by a concern for the future – but has also a stake in how the future is to be. It is with this dispute about the future and responsibility for the future that theology becomes political theology.

Bloch, like any other Marxist, is highly critical of the record of the church. But like many other Marxists he recognizes that the biblical faith has been overlaid and forgotten in such times. Through the Bible there are signs of a revolutionary potential too often suppressed and constantly a source of embarrassment to the authorities, civil and religious. 'The Bible has always been the church's bad conscience.' If he is critical of the church, Bloch still believes that the potential is still there in the tradition of biblical faith. Christians have within this tradition the resources by which to dispute the future for the sake of man.

The theology of hope is associated with the name of Jürgen Moltmann. As a young theologian Moltmann could not see how any advance could be made on the work of Barth. In the post-war period he could not become excited about the debate on existentialism and secularity provoked by Bultmann. His new theology began on reading the work of the Dutch Catholic writer Arnold van Ruler, in 1957, when his attention was drawn towards eschatology, mission and what he calls 'the joys of theological imagination'. Soon afterwards he read Bloch on the hope principle. He had no wish to compete with Bloch, but at once found the integration of his earlier interest in Old and New Testament (von Rad and Käsemann) with mission and a concern for the Kingdom of God. From Bloch he found himself recalled to the understanding of Christian faith as both world-transforming and world-overcoming. The God of the exodus and the God of the resurrection is a God who always goes on ahead. To be in Christ is to experience the future now and the new creation already begun.

Hope is not exhausted by the teaching on the life to come. It is also hope for this life. But in an evil world hope for this life means disputing the present and challenging the future. As he says in *Theology of Hope*, 'This is why faith, wherever it develops into hope, causes not rest but unrest, not patience but impatience. It does not calm the unquiet heart, but is itself this unquiet heart in man. Those who hope in Christ can no longer put up with reality as it is, but begin to suffer under it, to contradict it. Peace with God means conflict with the world ...'

Hope, therefore, is not another item to be dealt with by the dogmatic theologian. It is not something to be put to the end of the book as if it dealt only with 'the last things'. Nor is it the disposition of those who are comforted as they bear this life for the sake of a future life. The concern with hope does not leave the content of faith otherwise unchanged. For Moltmann it is such a crucial dimension of faith that it gives a perspective from which everything must be revised. When faith begins to hope then Christian theology becomes *spes quaerens intellectum*.

So far from having hope only for this life the history of Christianity has more often exhibited hope only for the life to come. This has led directly to indifference for this world and very often indifference to the conditions under which the vast majority of people live and die. But more than this, when there is no hope in this life faith is not fully tested out. Christian faith when inspired by hope claims to be more realistic than the realism of the world. It knows about evil and claims to

know how evil can be overcome. But Christian hope is not based
on naïve inexperience. (Moltmann's experience in Britain as a
prisoner of war should cause us to reflect on this point.) It does
not give rise to easy optimism but knows why it can move beyond
cynical pessimism. Hope for this world is not an optional extra
that some Christians might indulge in. Next to lack of love we must
place as the basic sin, lack of Christian hope. As Dante well knew,
hell begins where we abandon hope.

Jürgen Moltmann · *Meditation on Hope*

Jürgen Moltmann, *Theology of Hope*, SCM Press, London and Harper
& Row, NY 1967, pp.15-19, 21-22, 25-26, 324

Eschatology was long called the 'doctrine of the last things' or
the 'doctrine of the end'. By these last things were meant events
which will one day break upon man, history and the world at the
end of time. They included the return of Christ in universal glory,
the judgment of the world and the consummation of the kingdom,
the general resurrection of the dead and the new creation of all
things. These end events were to break into this world from somewhere beyond history, and to put an end to the history in which
all things here live and move. But the relegating of these events
to the 'last day' robbed them of their directive, uplifting and
critical significance for all the days which are spent here, this side
of the end, in history. Thus these teachings about the end led a
peculiarly barren existence at the end of Christian dogmatics. They
were like a loosely attached appendix that wandered off into
obscure irrelevancies. They bore no relation to the doctrines of
the cross and resurrection, the exaltation and sovereignty of Christ,
and did not derive from these by any logical necessity. They were
as far removed from them as All Souls' Day sermons are from
Easter. The more Christianity became an organization for disciple-
ship under the auspices of the Roman state religion and persistently
upheld the claims of that religion, the more eschatology and its
mobilizing, revolutionizing, and critical effects upon history as it
has now to be lived were left to fanatical sects and revolutionary
groups. Owing to the fact that Christian faith banished from its
life the future hope by which it is upheld, and relegated the future
to a beyond, or to eternity, whereas the biblical testimonies which
it handed on are yet full to the brim with future hope of a messianic

kind for the world, – owing to this, hope emigrated as it were from the Church and turned in one distorted form or another against the Church.

In actual fact, however, eschatology means the doctrine of the Christian hope, which embraces both the object hoped for and also the hope inspired by it. From first to last, and not merely in the epilogue, Christianity is eschatology, is hope, forward looking and forward moving, and therefore also revolutionizing and transforming the present. The eschatological is not one element *of* Christianity, but it is the medium of Christian faith as such, the key in which everything in it is set, the glow that suffuses everything here in the dawn of an expected new day. For Christian faith lives from the raising of the crucified Christ, and strains after the promises of the universal future of Christ. Eschatology is the passionate suffering and passionate longing kindled by the Messiah. Hence eschatology cannot really be only a part of Christian doctrine. Rather, the eschatological outlook is characteristic of all Christian proclamation, of every Christian existence and of the whole Church. There is therefore only one real problem in Christian theology, which its own object forces upon it and which it in turn forces on mankind and on human thought: the problem of the future. For the element of otherness that encounters us in the hope of the Old and New Testaments – the thing we cannot already think out and picture for ourselves on the basis of the given world and of the experiences we already have of that world – is one that confronts us with a promise of something new and with the hope of a future given by God. The God spoken of here is no intra-worldly or extra-worldly God, but the 'God of hope' (Rom. 15.13), a God with 'future as his essential nature' (as E. Bloch puts it), as made known in Exodus and in Israelite prophecy, the God whom we therefore cannot really have in us or over us but always only before us, who encounters us in his promises for the future, and whom we therefore cannot 'have' either, but can only await in active hope. A proper theology would therefore have to be constructed in the light of its future goal. Eschatology should not be its end, but its beginning.

But how can anyone speak of the future, which is not yet here, and of coming events in which he has not as yet had any part? Are these not dreams, speculations, longings and fears, which must all remain vague and indefinite because no one can verify them? The term 'eschato-*logy*' is wrong. There can be no 'doctrine' of the last things, if by 'doctrine' we mean a collection of theses which can be understood on the basis of experiences that constantly recur and are open to anyone. The Greek term *logos* refers to a reality which is there, now and always, and is given true expression in the word appropriate to it. In this sense there can be no *logos* of the future, unless the future is the continuation or regular recurrence of the present. If, however, the future were to bring something startlingly new, we have nothing to say of that, and nothing meaningful can be said of it either, for it is not in what is new and accidental, but only in things of an abiding and regularly recurring character that there can be log-ical truth. Aristotle, it is true, can call hope a 'waking dream', but for the Greeks it is nevertheless an evil out of Pandora's box.

But how, then, can Christian eschatology give expression to the future? Christian eschatology does not speak of the future as such. It sets out from a definite reality in history and announces the future of that reality, its future possibilities and its power over the future. Christian eschatology speaks of Jesus Christ and *his* future. It recognizes the reality of the raising of Jesus and proclaims the future of the risen Lord. Hence the question whether all statements about the future are grounded in the person and history of Jesus Christ provides it with the touchstone by which to distinguish the spirit of eschatology from that of utopia.

If, however, the crucified Christ has a future because of his resurrection, then that means on the other hand that all statements and judgments about him must at once imply something about the future which is to be expected from him. Hence the form in which Christian theology speaks of Christ cannot be the form of the Greek *logos* or of doctrinal statements based on experience, but only the form of statements of hope and of promises for the future. All predicates of Christ not only say who he was and is, but imply statements as to who he will be and what is to be expected from him. They all say: 'He is our hope' (Col. 1.27). In thus announcing his future in the world in terms of promise, they point believers in him towards the hope of his still outstanding future. Hope's statements of promise anticipate the future. In the promises, the hidden future already announces itself and exerts its influence on the present through the hope it awakens.

The truth of doctrinal statements is found in the fact that they can be shown to agree with the existing reality which we can all experience. Hope's statements of promise, however, must stand in contradiction to the reality which can at present be experienced. They do not result from experiences, but are the condition for the possibility of new experiences. They do not seek to illuminate the reality which exists, but the reality which is coming. They do not seek a mental picture of existing reality, but to lead existing reality towards the promised and hoped-for transformation. They do not seek to bear the train of reality, but to carry the torch before it. In so doing they give reality a historic character. But if reality is perceived in terms of history, then we have to ask with J. G. Hamann: 'Who would form proper concepts of the present without knowing the future?'

Present and future, experience and hope, stand in contradiction to each other in Christian eschatology, with the result that man is not brought into harmony and agreement with the given situation, but is drawn into the conflict between hope and experience. 'We are saved by hope. But hope that is seen is not hope; for what a man seeth, why doth he yet hope for? But if we hope for that we see not, then do we with patience wait for it' (Rom. 8.24, 25). Everywhere in the New Testament the Christian hope is directed towards what is not yet visible; it is consequently a 'hoping against hope' and thereby brands the visible realm of present experience as a god-forsaken, transient reality that is to be left behind. The contradiction to the existing reality of himself and his world in which man is placed by hope is the very contradiction out of which this hope itself is born – it is the contradiction between the resurrection and the cross. Christian hope is resurrection hope, and it proves its truth in the contradiction of the future prospects thereby offered and guaranteed for righteousness as opposed to sin, life as opposed to death, glory as opposed to suffering, peace as opposed to dissension. Calvin perceived very plainly the discrepancy involved in the resurrection hope: 'To us is given the promise of eternal life – but to us, the dead. A blessed resurrection is proclaimed to us – meantime we are surrounded by decay. We are called righteous – and yet sin lives in us. We hear of ineffable blessedness – but meantime we are here oppressed by infinite misery. We are promised abundance of all good things – yet we are rich only in hunger and thirst. What would become of us if we did not take our stand on hope, and if our heart did not hasten beyond this world through the midst of the darkness upon the path illumined by the word and Spirit of God!' (on Heb. 11.1).

It is in this contradiction that hope must prove its power. Hence eschatology, too, is forbidden to ramble, and must formulate its statements of hope in contradiction to our present experience of suffering, evil and death. For that reason it will hardly ever be possible to develop an eschatology on its own. It is much more important to present hope as the foundation and the mainspring of theological thinking as such, and to introduce the eschatological perspective into our statements on divine revelation, on the resurrection of Christ, on the mission of faith and on history.

But on the other hand, all this must inevitably mean that the man who thus hopes will never be able to reconcile himself with the laws and constraints of this earth, neither with the inevitability of death nor with the evil that constantly bears further evil. The raising of Christ is not merely a consolation to him in a life that is full of distress and doomed to die, but it is also God's contradiction of suffering and death, of humiliation and offence, and of the wickedness of evil. Hope finds in Christ not only a consolation *in* suffering, but also the protest of the divine promise *against* suffering. If Paul calls death the 'last enemy' (I Cor. 15.26), then the opposite is also true: that the risen Christ, and with him the resurrection hope, must be declared to be the enemy of death and of a world that puts up with death. Faith takes up this contradiction and thus becomes itself a contradiction to the world of death. That is why faith, wherever it develops into hope, causes not rest but unrest, not patience but impatience. It does not calm the unquiet heart, but is itself this unquiet heart in man. Those who hope in Christ can no longer put up with reality as it is, but begin to suffer under it, to contradict it. Peace with God means conflict with the world, for the goad of the promised future stabs inexorably into the flesh of every unfulfilled present. If we had before our eyes only what we see, then we should cheerfully or reluctantly reconcile ourselves with things as they happen to be. That we do not reconcile ourselves, that there is no pleasant harmony between us and reality, is due to our unquenchable hope. This hope keeps man unreconciled, until the great day of the fulfilment of all the promises of God. It keeps him *in statu viatoris*, in that unresolved openness to world questions which has its origin in the promise of God in the resurrection of Christ and can therefore be resolved only when the same God fulfils his promise. This hope makes the Christian Church a constant disturbance in human society, seeking as the latter does to stabilize itself into a 'continuing city'. It makes the Church the source of continual new impulses towards the realization of righteousness, freedom and humanity here in the light of the promised future that is to come. This Church is committed to 'answer for the hope' that is in it (I Peter 3.15). It is called in question 'on account of the hope and resurrection of the dead' (Acts 23.6). Wherever that happens, Christianity embraces its true nature and becomes a witness of the future of Christ.

*   *   *

Hope alone is to be called 'realistic', because it alone takes seriously the possibilities with which all reality is fraught. It does not take things as they happen to stand or to lie, but as progressing, moving things with possibilities of change. Only as long as the world and the people in it are in a fragmented and experimental state which is not yet resolved, is there any sense in earthly hopes. The latter anticipate what is possible to reality, historic and moving as it is, and use their influence to decide the processes of history. Thus hopes and anticipations of the future are not a transfiguring glow superimposed upon a darkened existence, but are realistic ways of perceiving the scope of our real possibilities, and as such they set everything in motion and keep it in a state of change. Hope and the kind of thinking that goes with it consequently cannot submit to the reproach of being utopian, for they do not strive after things that have 'no place', but after things that have 'no place *as yet*' but can acquire one. On the other hand, the celebrated realism of the stark facts, of established objects and laws, the attitude that despairs of its possibilities and clings to reality as it is, is inevitably much more open to the charge of being utopian, for in its eyes there is 'no place' for possibilities, for future novelty, and consequently for the historic character of reality. Thus the despair which imagines it has reached the end of its tether proves to be illusory, as long as nothing has yet come to an end but everything is still full of possibilities. Thus positivistic realism also proves to be illusory, so long as the world is not a fixed body of facts but a network of paths and processes, so long as the world does not only run according to laws but these laws themselves are also flexible, so long as it is a realm in which necessity means the possible, but not the unalterable.

Statements of hope in Christian eschatology must also assert themselves against the rigidified utopia of realism, if they would keep faith alive and would guide obedience in love on to the path towards earthly, corporeal, social reality. In its eyes the world is full of all kinds of possibilities, namely all the possibilities of the God of hope. It sees reality and mankind in the hand of him whose voice calls into history from its end, saying, 'Behold, I make all things new', and from hearing this word of promise it acquires the freedom to renew life here and to change the face of the world.

The theological 'self-understanding' (*Selbstverständnis*) of the Christian faith always stands in a relation to the socially 'axiomatic' (*Selbstverständliche*). Only where we become critically aware of this connection can the symbiosis be resolved and the peculiar character of the Christian faith come to expression in conflict with the things that are socially axiomatic. If Christianity, according to the will of him in whom it believes and in whom it hopes, is to be different and to serve a different purpose, then it must address itself to no less a task than that of breaking out of these its socially fixed roles. It must then display a kind of conduct which is not in accordance with these. That is the conflict which is imposed on every Christian and every Christian minister. If the God who called them to life should expect of them something other than what modern industrial society expects and requires of them, then Christians must venture an exodus and regard their social roles as a new Babylonian exile. Only where they appear in society as a group which is not wholly adaptable and in the case of which the modern integration of everything with everything else fails to succeed, do they enter into a conflict-laden, but fruitful partnership with this society. Only where their resistance shows them to be a group that is incapable of being assimilated or of 'making the grade', can they communicate their own hope to this society. They will then be led in this society to a constant unrest which nothing can allay or bring to accommodation and rest. Here the task of Christianity today is not so much to oppose the ideological glorification of things, but rather to resist the institutional stabilizing of things, and by 'raising the question of meaning' to make things uncertain and keep them moving and elastic in the process of history. This aim – here formulated to begin with in very general terms – is not achieved simply by stirring up 'historicality', vitality and mobility in the realms which are socially unburdened but have been brought socially to general stagnation. It is achieved precisely by breaking through this social stagnation. Hope alone keeps life – including public, social life – flowing and free.

Josef Pieper · *Hope and History*

Josef Pieper, *Hope and History*, Burns & Oates, London and Herder & Herder, NY 1969, pp.61-68. © 1969 by Burns & Oates Ltd. Used by permission of the publisher, The Seabury Press

The most forceful statements on the theme of 'hope', the broadest as well as the deepest analysis in contemporary writing, is undoubtedly to be found in the work of Ernst Bloch. The subject which has engaged his intense interest for nearly fifty years of literary activity is expressed in the title of his early book, *Geist der Utopie* ('Spirit of Utopia'), written in 1918. In the author's note to the 1963 re-issue of this book he explicitly affirms the continuity of his subject-matter through all the works published in the interval, up to the voluminous and conclusive book he wrote in exile, *Daz Prinzip Hoffnung* ('The Principle of Hope'). The identity and unity of this underlying idea, however, produces anything but monotony. We need only skim the table of contents in his book on hope, and leaf casually through its pages to notice the unexpected and almost overwhelming variety and abundance of concrete detail he discusses: the fantasies of children playing hide-and-seek, the new dress in a lighted shop window, the happy ending of entertainment movies, Mozart operas, social utopias from Plato to Marx, the wishful architecture of fairy-tales, the celestial rose of Dante's *Commedia*; Mignon's nostalgic song, Don Quixote, the Bach fugue, Lao-tse, Confucius, Buddha, Mohammed – all the way to Marxism's acclaim of the realm of freedom. The whole, moreover, is written in a totally jargon-free, humanly direct language inspired by passionate concern with the subject. From the first moment on (and especially in the first moment) the reader is fascinated by the sonority and polyphony of Bloch's diction; this is not the kind of prose one is accustomed to find in philosophical writings. That very fact, to be sure, suggests the reverse of the medal. It is definitely not easy to discover what, on the whole and in detail, is really being asserted. This difficulty even affects the principal ideas, including that of 'hope' itself. 'Weaving music in the tunnel of the soul' – Ernst Bloch uses this phrase from Hegel to characterize in retrospect his own early work. It is, however, equally apt for the major book on hope which he wrote late in life. In it, by way of defining the object of hope, he offers a list of other things which to him are more or less synonyms: 'Happiness, freedom, non-alienation, Golden Age, land of milk and honey, the eternal feminine, the trumpet signal in *Fidelio*, the Christlike aspect of the coming Resurrection Day.' Yes, Bloch's language is indeed as 'dream-coloured' as it has been termed. But because of this highly praised quality, it becomes almost impossible to couch his fundamental ideas in the form of a summary, and to discuss them critically. Nevertheless I must make the attempt.

Bloch likes to refer to his *opus* as an 'encyclopedia', a comprehensive account of the images of man's hopes, an effort to formulate just what is hoped for in human hopes. This is in fact the most persuasive aspect of his undertaking, and at the same time the one that raises fewest problems. Let us therefore consider it first. Bloch himself says that he is concerned with interpreting 'the dreams of the better life'. What, then, do men mean by 'the better life', or as Bloch rings changes on the phrase, the 'perfect' life, the 'full' life and 'full existence'. They mean: 'the world without disappointment'; 'reaching home'; a 'joy like no other that has ever been'; 'all needs being met'; 'peace, freedom, bread'; 'heaven on earth'; 'the world as man's homeland'; 'the world becoming like a house'; 'restoration of man'; a world in which 'man is a man to men' and not a wolf; *regnum humanum*; 'enlightened man at one with an enlightened world.'

As I have said, this encyclopedic inventory is the least questionable aspect of Bloch. Nevertheless, there are a few doubts here, too. We need only look at the obvious omissions or emphases. The last-named item, for example ('enlightened man at one with an enlightened world')—this, says Bloch, is 'the most hoped for of all that men hope, called the highest good'; it is the 'all' which in the past was conceived 'mythologically as heaven'. Naturally, man's coming into his own and his harmony with a perfected world can be interpreted in a variety of ways. I myself could easily understand this phraseology as a description of Eternal Bliss; I could say the same about the other, somewhat unusual, tag about 'all needs being met'. Why not? But Bloch is determined to rule out any such interpretation; his inventory itself is limited to those aspects of hopes that are, as he puts it, 'non-illusory'. To be sure, he does not hesitate to speak on occasion of the 'kingdom of heaven' and 'attaining bliss'; but he means exclusively 'heaven *on earth*'. He even, like Kant, speaks of the 'kingdom of God', but of a 'kingdom of God – without God'. The biblical concept of the 'kingdom' is another of his basic and recurrent concepts; but 'the utopia of the kingdom' is 'based on the assumption that no God remains in the heavens, since there is none there and never was'. 'The world has no beyond'; and 'the fixed point high above [is] precisely the falsehood'. Although this last is quite correctly directed against the Enlightenment's Deistic notion of an 'extramundane God' which the mainstream of Occidental theology rejects just as forcibly as Ernst Bloch – nevertheless this consistently asserted atheism of course applies to any possible conception of deity.

What, then, is the situation? Questions arise with the very first step: the endeavour to draw up a comprehensive inventory of the hopes actually cherished by men becomes difficult. For Bloch would limit this list to those hopes which are indeed realizable in this world. Everything else is dismissed from consideration as 'illusory'. Incidentally, Bloch is quite right in one respect: We can wish for the most impossible things, but can hope only for what is possible. But who is going to determine what is 'possible' and what is not? Christendom, at any rate – and Christendom after all has an empirical existence – insists (indeed its content is) that it is not illusory to hope for an 'eternal life', for the 'Resurrection of the Dead', and also for 'Heaven', simply that, neither more nor less. But Bloch's catalogue, though multifarious enough in other respects, says nothing at all about these hopes. We should not quarrel with him, however, before we have gone a bit deeper and discussed several antecedent and even more fundamental questions.

Ernst Bloch is not content merely to argue that man's hope, insofar as it really deserves the name, is exclusively concerned with things attainable in this world. Beyond that, he is convinced that these hopes can be attained solely by 'socialistic transformation of the world'. 'The dreams of the better life have always postulated a happiness that only Marxism can lead to.' 'Everything non-illusionary in the images of hope comes down to Marx.' Marxism is 'the salvation of the sound core of utopia'; it is 'attainment of humanity'.

I consider it highly valuable to hear Bloch's opinions on the future shape of the world, on the impossibility of a purely 'static concept of being', and on the 'ontology of the not-yet-existent'. If we listen closely we may comprehend anew the old Occidental wisdom, now so often forgotten, of the concept of 'viatoric existence'. But we must not lose sight of the fact that for Bloch these are merely preliminaries. For he is not an advocate of Marxism merely as an 'idea' or of socialism as a kind of *weltanschauung*, a matter which undoubtedly could provide material for ample discussion. Who, incidentally, would not be a 'socialist' if socialism consisted in nothing more than the goal of having men behave like men towards other men, and not like wolves? Bloch, however, is committed to Marxism as a political reality. Not that this cannot also be the subject of 'discussion', but let us be quite clear what we are discussing.

Bloch, then, speaks explicitly of 'those countries in which Marxism has become the power'. In them alone, he says, 'the daydream of the *regnum humanum* no longer exists in the air or in heaven'. He is unmistakably saying that in the Soviet Union there is beginning to be achieved what Joachim of Fiore meant by the Third Kingdom[1] – which, however, 'the darkness comprehendeth not'. And nowhere except in 'the building of Communism' does 'the content of the realm of freedom' enter into its first realization; before this, it has 'nowhere been present'. Curiously enough the most extreme formulation of this idea is to be found in the section of Bloch's book which deals with the political role of Jewry in the world. Bloch explicitly describes this role as ethical, if not quite religious. Jewry signifies 'not only a more or less anthropological quality ... but also a certain messianic affect, a nostalgia for the true Canaan'. 'The only question involved is this : have the Jews ... still, as such, an awareness of what the God of the Exodus said to his servant Israel, not as a promise but as an assignment: "I have put my spirit upon him, he will bring forth justice to the gentiles." ' Only in terms of this description can we understand how Bloch can say that, of all things, the realistic aspect, the 'utterly unsentimental' aspect of hope is expressed in the words of the psalm (Ps. 137.5): 'If I forget you, O Jerusalem, let my right hand wither!' Though we might well ask where in these words is there any foreshadowing of atheism or of imprisonment within the experiences of this world? Nevertheless, in a fervent polemic against Zionism and incidentally also against the State of Israel, Bloch takes this great mystic name 'Jerusalem' and with no more ado attaches it to the political foundations of Marxism: 'What elements of the prophetic heritage live on in Judaism and alone make it important ... have been given present-day meaning ... by Marx.' And now follows that extreme formulation with which I am here concerned, that incredible identification of Jerusalem with Lenin: *'Ubi Lenin, ibi Jerusalem!'*

It seems to me that there cannot be a more aggressive, plainer and in a certain sense more shocking avowal of the conviction that everything man can meaningfully hope for, everything inner experience and tradition have taught him to hope for, the complete sum of what can be hoped for and is worth hoping for, must be attained in this world and that, moreover, such attainment ultimately depends entirely on political and social activity, to be exact on that 'socialist transformation of the world' which has already begun in Marxist revolution.

---

[1] The author uses the ambiguous German term which can also signify 'Third Reich.'

Rubem A. Alves · *The Dialectics of Freedom*

The Historicity of Freedom

The reason why Christians and political humanists find themselves so often together in common tasks is that the languages they speak spring from a similar passion and point to a similar hope. Both languages could be described as expressive of a 'passion for and vision of human deliverance' (P. Lehmann). What separates them is the basic historical experience in which they were formed and which determines the understanding of the context that makes possible the transformation of this vision and passion into historical reality.

In the preceding analysis of the language of political humanism we indicated that it is thoroughly historical. It is born out of the experience of the pains of the world, its contradictions and negativity. It points to a historical future of humanization, in which the possibilities of human liberation that are arrested by and in the present could become historical. And finally we indicated that it is a language of freedom because it negates and hopes to the extent to which it believes that man is free and powerful enough to liberate himself from what keeps him under bondage. The language of political humanism is therefore a form of historical optimism. It takes the risk of making all its hopes for a new future for man depend on man's freedom to make history free. The passion for and vision of human liberation will become historical 'by the powers of man alone' (ibid.). Humanization is man's task. It is a form of optimism that combines a confidence in man's vocation for freedom, his determination to create a new future, and a confidence in the openness of history to this activity of man. It believes that 'mankind always sets itself only such problems as it can solve; for when we look closer we will always find that the problem itself only arises when the material conditions for its solution are already present or at least in the process of coming into being.' Man's openness to the future is thus the indication that the future is open to him, ripe for his action. Therefore the emergence of the consciousness of 'ought' coincides with the subjective and objective possibility of the 'can.'

The problem which the language of political humanism presents, however, is whether it is possible to remain thoroughly historical and optimistic at the same time. Can this optimism as to man, as the only creator of history, survive when confronted with the brutal fact of power in our present-day world? ...

It seems to me that this is indeed a realistic assessment of our present situation. Nothing indicates that the horizons are becoming more open. On the contrary: the openness of consciousness and its emergence in history is being overcome by the repressive powers of conservatism. We live indeed amid the contradiction between the reality and impossibility of a new tomorrow. It is real as a dimension of consciousness, but it is impossible because of the exercise of power on the part of the dominating systems. 'Humanistic messianism' and its passion for and vision of human deliverance by the powers of man alone is confronted thus with the alternative between, on the one hand, optimism at the expense of its thoroughly historical character, becoming thus romantic, and, on the other, faithfulness to history and the abandonment of hope, becoming then prey to cynicism generated by frustration.

The language spoken by the community of faith, although dominated by the same vision of and passion for human deliverance, finds a different context for its negation, hope, and action, because it 'insists that the achievement of humanization comes by the reality and power of a deliverance which occurs in history from beyond history and refuses to abandon history' (ibid). In other words: for messianic humanism the politics for a new tomorrow cannot be assessed by a simple statistical or quantitative evaluation of the human resources and of the power of resistance of the existing structures of domination. It holds that the politics for a new tomorrow is the business of a power which, being free from history, and therefore not being exhausted by the statistical-quantitative possibilities that history displays, is 'free for' history and therefore creates possibilities which could not be dreamed of by means of calculation.

The fact that the biblical communities were created and determined by liberating historical events led them to have a unique understanding of history, as the history of freedom. As we indicated before, the experience of historical events as formative and liberating did not allow the community of faith simply to see them as the result of accident or circumstance. They were acts, that is, events determined by freedom and therefore events which bore freedom in themselves. They presented, consequently, new exits from the enclosed circle of 'what was,' new openings towards different historical possibilities. Time, therefore, ceased to be considered simply as the continuum of the system of natural causality and became the creation of the will. God's will created time, it created the 'ultimate ground of man's life.' 'But will by its nature is future-regarding, future-seeking, future-creating' (P. Minear). The time created by this future-determined will is thus the time of a project. But project means to emerge from identity with 'what is.' It means both will's freedom from the power of the world of the present and will's freedom for a new future to be created. To be involved in God's time is thus to participate in a present that determines itself for the creation of a new tomorrow. The will of God could never, therefore, be invoked in order to justify the status quo. 'It is the will of God,' says the religious man, adjusting himself to his captivity. The will of God is here the justification of what is. It explains the necessity of what is by referring it to the divine causality and to the divine reconciliation of the historical contradictions. When the language of messianic humanism refers to the will of God, however, it is rather indicating that because time expresses the pressure of the spirit, of freedom, as it seeks its goal, it can never be stopped. Therefore, every present must be experienced as time-towards-the-new-tomorrow. The new tomorrow is thus the sole determination of the present.

The Dialectics of Freedom

Humanistic messianism and messianic humanism are both dominated by the love and vision of human deliverance. Human deliverance, however, is not yet historical, it cannot be found as a reality in the present. It exists now as a project of the will. Therefore, it can be expressed only in the language of hope, in the universe of discourse which speaks not about the actual in history but about that which is possible to history. For both of them, therefore, the alternative, hope without history and history without hope, are equally abominable, since they mean that human liberation is impossible in history. The project of human liberation and with it both humanistic messianism and messianic humanism would thus be proved to be nonsense, since the language of human liberation is meaningful only if it refers to a project born out of history and which is possible in history. In other words: hope has to be the language of the possible, if it is to inform and determine ethics as the science and activity that aims at the historization of hope. Hope therefore cannot be confused with fantasy or illusion, because it is derived from history and envisions, from the experience of the past, what is possible to history. It is the extrapolation into the future of man's historical experience with the politics of freedom in the past. In hope reason does not play the function of describing 'what is.' It is no longer 'conformed to this world' but rather free for the criticism of 'what is' for the sake of that which could be. Consequently, 'hope alone is to be called "realistic," ' observes Moltmann, 'because it alone takes seriously the possibilities with which all reality is fraught. It does not take things as they happen to stand or to lie, but as progressing, moving things with possibilities of change.... [Hope is thus] a realistic way of perceiving the scope of our real possibilities.' Reason dominated by hope sees the real through the experience with the liberating activity of freedom in the world, as a politics which 'gives life to the dead and calls into existence the things that do not exist' (Rom. 4.17). The real is that which, through freedom, can be. For reason without hope the real is the brute reality of 'what is' as the ultimate datum of its experience. It does not make room, therefore, for the activity that aims at overcoming the inhuman of 'what is' in order to create a new and more human reality. Hope, consequently, expresses what is possible to history and therefore what can be made historical through the activity of freedom, only to the extent to which it is derived from and is an extrapolation of the objective movement of the politics of human liberation, as experienced in history. In other words: it is not enough to say that freedom opens its way towards the future in history; hope emerges when we are able to see how freedom moves on its way. Only thus does it serve ethics. Only thus is it a realistic way of perceiving history.

For the sake of hope and human liberation it is therefore of the utmost importance to unmask the pseudo-hopes, visions of the future that are not derived from the reading of the objective movement of the politics of freedom in history. Visions of the future not extracted from history or which do not take the movement of freedom as their basis, cannot be called hope: they are forms of alienation, illusions which cannot inform history because of their unrelatedness to the way of operation of freedom in the world.

This is one of the reasons why humanistic messianism maintains a polemic with religion: it offers to man a hope not derived from history, a hope that hovers above and beyond history, and which is not mediated through the activity of freedom in history. Because it is not extracted from history it does not point to what is historically possible. Instead of making man free for history, it rather uproots him from it. Hope would be here a compensation for the impotence of freedom and the expression of man's despair of the possibilities of history. It would be a creation of the inability of man's subjectivity to come to terms with its own frustrations, but not the result of its experience with the objective liberating movement of freedom.

Humanistic messianism and messianic humanism have as well a polemic with the idea of progress and the hope it implies. This is rather strange, because it seems that there is no hope that could claim to be as based on historical facts and more faithful to what is possible to history than presented by the idea of progress. The modern idea of progress is the result of an extrapolation of the experience of the emergence of reason in history, as the man of the Enlightenment understood it. Mankind had reached a stage in which reason finally disentangled itself from the irrational and instinctive. Free from the irrational, reason was believed to be the lord of history. There was the future of man, like a block of marble, waiting to be given a shape according to the verdict of reason as to what was right. From the historical experience of the liberation of reason, man then turned his eyes to the future and was able to envisage the new world he was now free to create. It is true that this naïve optimism has been to a great extent destroyed by the historical experiences of our century. But not completely, because now, as never before, the same spirit of optimism as to progress has become embodied in technological reason, as the messianism of technology, as technologism. From the point of view of the messianism of technology the world lies wide open ahead of man, simply waiting for the 'technique' that will make his hopes historical reality. It cannot say that it does not possess any 'concepts which could bridge the gap between the present and the future.' It knows how to do it. It believes, therefore, that ideology is no longer necessary as a tool for the creation of the future. Bondage is overcome by wisdom and knowledge.

The problem with the messianism of technology and the idea of progress, from the perspective of the historical experience of humanistic messianism and messianic humanism, is that the rationality operative in technology is not derived from the experience with the liberating movement of freedom in history but rather from the rationality of nature. It makes room for the quantitatively different but not for the qualitatively new. It is a rationality that depends on quantitative changes to survive but dies if qualitative changes occur. Progress or economic development, as the creation of technology, would thus become a different sort of opiate that would prevent qualitative changes, changes created by freedom, by making freedom tamed through the marvels and power of the quantitative factor. It would make freedom domesticated, thereby destroying it as freedom. It would make the sphere of what is possible to history shrink to what is allowed by the technological system. Because this vision of hope is not extracted from the history of freedom but rather from the paradigm of nature, history, as the history of freedom, comes to an end.

The hope of human liberation, the hope for the qualitatively new, the hope which is to be the child of freedom, can be thought of only when one discovers how freedom in the past has mediated the new and liberating to history.

Messianic humanism and humanistic messianism cannot therefore accept any type of hope save the hope that is concretely derived from their vision of the how of freedom in history, of the way whereby it is able to overcome the old and enslaving and thereby make room for the new and liberating. And the historical experience of both of them indicates one thing: freedom creates the new in history through a dialectical process. The new is not mediated directly. The reason for this is that the old, in history, resists and opposes the new. As a consequence, the Yes that freedom addresses to the new becomes historical only through and beyond the No with which it confronts, resists, and overcomes the power of the old that wants to perpetuate itself and abort the new...

The possibility of liberation and the shape of hope is thus derived from the perception of the conflicting character of the process whereby freedom opens its way towards the new. The movement can be summarized in three moments:

First: the reality of the old as power used for self-preservation, against the new, as violence.

Second: freedom as power against the violence of preservation, as the negation of the negative.

Third: freedom as power for creation of the new, for experimentation, as affirmation.

Humanistic messianism and messianic humanism thus agree not only in their common passion for and vision of human liberation but also as to the dynamics whereby freedom mediates this hope into history. Again what separates them is the basic historical experience that formed them. They hope, therefore, from a different assessment of what it is that is possible to freedom, and therefore of what it is that is possible to history.

Humanistic messianism sees the dialectic of freedom as intrinsically and exclusively determined by the dialectic of the material relations in society. Consequently, only to the extent that man suffers the contradictions of the material relations and consciously becomes aware of this contradiction does he emerge as the power that negates in order to overcome. In this context, he has a free consciousness committed to the project of transforming its hope of liberation in historical reality. He is the revolutionary. Human liberation is thus the creation of the powers of man alone, and the historization of hope depends exclusively on the determination of his will. However, present-day technological society confronts man with two new elements: first, its ability to overcome the material contradictions of society, if not actually at least virtually. It displays, therefore, the power of eliminating opposition, of eliminating the pain of the contradictions. The goods it distributes function as the opiate of the people. It thus makes consciousness unable to say 'No.' And second, it has concentrated in the hands of the masters such a massive amount of power that it seems that they are now able to destroy the negative powers of society. The dragon devours the lion. The hope of humanistic messianism, consequently, faces the danger of collapse. Humanistic messianism is then confronted with the options that are the negation of itself: hope without history or history without hope. By the powers of man alone man hopes without confidence: 'nothing indicates that the end will be a good end.' There is no promise that freedom will succeed in its painful dialectical movement towards man's liberation. It is in this context that the historical experience of messianic humanism with the dialectics of freedom offers a different assessment of what is possible to history, thereby providing a different ground for the hope of human liberation.

3 · Theology of Revolution

By the late 1960s a new kind of political theology was clearly emerging. It was stimulated by contact with neo-Marxist thought, especially the humanist dimensions of the young Marx. But it is important to emphasize that whether in personal dialogue or in more systematic study there was no temptation to substitute Marx for Christ. The first gain was in a fundamental reassessment of the form in which Christian faith had happily existed for so long in an evil world. The second gain was, if anything, more important.

One of the most important influences on Marx was the work of Feuerbach. Marx considered him to be one of the most creative critical thinkers of the age. Yet to the last he was a thinker, and Marx was forced to bring this criticism against him. 'The philosophers have only interpreted the world, in various ways : the point is to change it.' This thesis was originally directed against the Hegelians and their rather touching faith in the effectiveness of correct conceptualization. But the thesis applies more widely and equally describes theologians – whether theologians of hope or not – who stop at making theological assertions about the world.

It is not enough to have a division of labour in which some men interpret the world and others act upon it. In the light of what Marx said about *praxis*, it is clear that philosophers cannot expect to reach a correct interpretation of the world unless they become involved in the process of engaging with the world. Christians should not be unfamiliar with this idea that until we do the truth we cannot come to any further truth, but rather risk losing the truth we thought we possessed.

The theology of hope makes fine reading, but it must be put into practice. Much of the subsequent writing on the theology of hope lacks credibility for precisely this reason. Yet theologians, in common with other academics, always want to do just a little bit more to finalize their interpretation of the world. A theologian writing massive volumes on dogmatics can spend all day in the library, controlling his subject completely. The trouble arises when theology turns its attention to the on-going movement of the world and begins to enter a dispute about the future. Then theologians find that they cannot control their subject. The world will neither stand still nor passively slip into ready-made theological costume.

In the case of political theology the time is not of our choosing, the occasion is never the right one and the categories do not fit well. But suddenly the challenge comes to act on our good works or retire to the library. The year was 1968, the action was the French student demonstrations and the interpretation was revolution. Theology is mostly concerned with history, and theologians make confident statements about how the people of God acted in ancient times. But was everything quite so clear to those involved in ambiguous situations? In 1968 there came a time for *praxis*, the time of taking risks in a very complex situation. It was a time for testing faith, or retiring to the library till everything became clear and settled.

All credit to Moltmann that, respectable theologian that he was, he was prepared to commit himself. 'The new criterion of theology and of faith is to be found in action.' (How had we ever come to think that the criterion of theology lay in its conformity to the past?) The issue, of course, was not this or that student demand in Paris or Madrid. The issue was about the future and how it is to look. The issue was about how the present is determined and who is to determine how things will be. In so far as higher education is a very important factor in shaping the future, for good or ill, then inevitably the place of the universities in all this was crucial. It is unfortunate, however, that the original dimensions of the issue were quickly lost sight of, and the whole matter reduced to questions of university government. For example, Daniel Cohn-Bendit was associated in the minds of many with student politics. Yet in his book *Obsolete Communism* (itself an indication of the rejection of Stalinism on the left) he could claim that 'Revolution is not about a change in management, but a change in man'. Frantz Fanon in *The Wretched of the Earth*, rediscovered about this time, had written of the war in Algeria, 'Total liberation is that which concerns all sectors of the personality'. Che Guevara, that other saint of the revolutionary left, had described the work of the guerrilla forces in the villages. 'We spoke to the people about their lives, and *that* was the revolution.' In 1968 this most fundamental question was being brought out on to the streets where it became more than an interpretation and debating point. What is the nature of man? What are the factors in society which prevent fulfilment in the very broadest sense?

This was an issue to bring joy to Christian ears, to hear such questions from the lips of those previously classified as materialists. In the event, it transpired that materialism did not belong to Marxists but to the organizers of the affluent society with its over-heated consumptive economy and to the house-trained prophets and baptizers thereof. Nor was this fundamental question restricted to the young European left: it had already been asked four years earlier in Berkeley, in an institution of American affluence. This great refusal on the part of the heirs of affluence gladdened the heart of Herbert Marcuse who in *One Dimensional Man* described the loss of transcendence, the impoverishment of life and the subtle constraints which lead back to conformity and death. 'It is a good way of life – much better than before – and as a good way of life, it militates against qualitative change.' That generation would have inherited the world – and lost their soul. It was all there in the biblical faith: why had the theologians failed to teach it and the church to practise it?

So it was that in trying to respond to the challenge of interpreta-tion and *praxis* the theology of hope became better described as the theology of revolution. Christian faith which thinks it can dispute the present and challenge the future by advocating marginal changes in personal behaviour fails to realize the power and persistence of non-Christian values which have been entrenched and institutionalized in our dominant culture. The Beatitudes represent the foundations of a revolutionary new society which has never appeared in history and towards which no culture is moving, gradually or inevitably. Evolution does not lead to the kingdom of God.

But things reverted to normal, that peace which only the world can give, and church and state drank a toast on the day it was announced that the revolution will not now take place. Yet as Donald Schon has pointed out, 'normal' now must be taken to mean steady and inevitable change. We shall never know stability again. People must now be trained for change and be taught to live in a culture where change is a permanent feature of life. The revolutionaries know this already: 'revolution in the revolution' means that revolution is not an event, a goal achieved. It is a permanent way of life which prevents today's breakthrough from becoming tomorrow's constraint. But should this not be the environment of a reformed theology which holds *ecclesia reformata semper reformanda*?

Tillich could say that theology must be done again in every

age. But what of theology in our age, of which Moltmann claims 'we shall increasingly experience history as revolution'? Our fathers in the faith spent their energies in finding the appropriate expression of faith for their time. We do our contemporaries a disservice if we spend our energies lovingly reconstructing the theologies of an age quite different from our own. The theology for our age has yet to be written, or as Moltmann puts it, there will be no ' "theology of revolution" until there is a revolution in theology'.

Trutz Rendtorff · *Conflict between Enlightenment and Orthodoxy*

Trutz Rendtorff, *Theologie der Revolution. Analysen und Materialien*, section 111, pp.67-75. Translated by John Bowden. © 1968 by Suhrkamp Verlag, Frankfurt am Main.

A consideration of the course of the theology of revolution (as far as that has been possible hitherto), its structure and its theological arguments, reveals a remarkable ambivalence. This arises from the association of political and social progressiveness with the tendencies of an ultimately uncritical theology of the Bible and history. The material importance of the political and social problems of which revolutionary theology makes itself the spokesman cannot be contested. But if one considers it as theology, and asks the question whether in the long run these problems can be incorporated into such a theology and can thus be universalized, this ambivalence must offer food for thought. Without question, this theology understands itself to derive its impetus and impact from the revolutionary perspective of social reality. But it seeks to do justice to this reality as theology in a way which produces very direct relationships with particular elements of the religious tradition of Christianity and is essentially the characteristic of pre-critical theology.

Yet what might at first sight appear to be a lack of productive theological originality, and might incur the criticism of being well-meaning practice which tends to run ahead of theory, is not just conditioned fortuitously and locally. The conception is developed by means of the model of *two theologies*, one of which is devoted to the individual salvation of man, his faith and his worship of God, and is regarded as that of the existing church, whereas the other has as its content involvement for man, the fellowship of

Christians with each other and with God (*koinonia*) and participation in the historical action of God. This is the context in
which it sets out to be theology of revolution. Thus the principal
model in the structure of this theology is that of the opposition
between old and new society. It repeats itself in respect of theological thinking and determines the choice of themes. Such
conceptualization follows the thesis that every theology also always
includes a whole world. The analysis of this involvement in the
world is the critical element here, especially where there is reflection on the consequence that a theology acquires stability through
its social dimension, whether this is conscious or unconscious. It
is from here that it draws its constructive power, by using the
political and sociological implications of theology as a means for
its own development.

The shape and content of this theology are also governed by a
quite different opposition, which feeds on developments which
have become the characteristic of twentieth-century theology along
a broad front. As is well known, starting from Germany theology
has begun to break with its modern traditions since the twenties,
and on the whole influential features of this development seem
to be recurring in the theology of revolution. Criticism has referred
to the uncertainty of a definition of theology and faith which
begins from man in his individual sphere and finds its limits of
interpretation within that framework. Above all, and in more
general terms, criticism was directed towards putting theology
under the conditions of the modern period and setting limits to
the claim to totality which it had made in earlier times. This
criticism evidently recurs in the model of the two theologies. The
theology of revolution also follows the process of theology's newly-
awakened claim to totality which contests the modern humanization and limitation of Christian theology in the name of the
sovereignty of God. Seen in this context within theology, and as
theology, the theology of revolution is the newest form of the
attempt to help theology once again to secure a total, all-
embracing significance. This can only happen when not only the
old dogmatic but also the new social dimension, which goes
beyond individuality, is opened up to it. The revolutionary orientation then becomes a means of liberating theology from all those
limitations of the modern period which have in fact led to a crisis
in dogmatic theology. There are reasons *within* theology for an
alliance with a revolutionary approach which is motivated in other
ways. For criticism of modern society has always been in the
interests of theology. Only in the conjunction of biblical eschatology

with social and political revolution does the theology of the word of God find its corresponding relationship with the world. The theologoumenon of the word of revelation as a total transformation of the world and of man is thus apparently freed from obscure dialectic where it finds expression in the postulate of a new world and society. In alliance with revolution in society, theology unburdens itself of the need to set out and prove its own claim in the context of Christianity and its world as they now are. The essential dilemmas of dialectical theology seem easier to overcome where they are loaded on to a disappearing world. This indication of the wider context in which the theology of revolution must be seen cannot be omitted. For the alliance of theology with revolution must be named, to leave open the possibility that theology can view social and political problems in quite a different way from that adopted by the theology of revolution.

This situation becomes clear in the reversal which takes place in the implementation of the theology of revolution and is part of its ambivalence. After going through the criticism of existing Christianity and present society, it sets itself above such a reality. If it is regarded in a systematic way, its major premise is 'God's action in history', as the constantly recurring formula has it. As a theologoumenon, this formula frees that to which it refers from the existing state of affairs: that is the reason why it has been coined. At the same time, however, it also removes it from any theoretical criticism, since *this* reality of the divine action in history is no longer reached by reflective criticism because it is at the same time the major premise of all criticism. This major premise is communicated in the *koinonia* of those who place themselves in the unlimited and illimitable movement of a changing action of the God of history. The goal and content of this movement and this fellowship is permanent humanization. In this way the starting point of the problem is reached again: the humanity of man, which cannot fully be realized.

We can only touch on the connection between the theology of revolution which we have investigated and the outline of ethics given by Paul Lehmann in his book *Ethics in a Christian Context*. In this context Richard Shaull certainly plays an important role as mediator. Lehmann's outline represents an attempt to develop something like an Aristotelian ethic of the *polis* in the circumstances of a Christian outline of history. The place of the institution of the *polis*, to which Aristotle looks back and in which human freedom is realized, is taken by the context of the divine action in history in which humanization can be achieved. This context is revolutionary because it exists only in God's action, on which no one can look back, because it brings in the end itself. For Lehmann's theological outline this context of divine history is the limiting framework of ethics, taking over the function which the *polis* has in Aristotle. But if this context is grounded in the divine action, ethics cannot and may not be a determination of ethical subjectivity, and in that case Lehmann's criticism is directed against it also. Thus the *Christian Context*, the theology of history, competes with the modern world. Here the determination of ethics in the Kantian sense took the place of that world-system in which theological theory also involved moral action; the freedom and autonomy of the ethical subject correspond to the aporia of theoretical knowledge. Viewed in this way the theology of history which gives ethics its context is the attempt to remove the grounds which have made ethics necessary in modern times, i.e. to outline another world in which ethics can and should once again follow the example which has been gained from the theological knowledge of history.

If in Lehmann the revolutionary movement is a category of historicity, distinct from the stability of the *polis* ethic, in Shaull and the theology of revolution which follows him it is the category of practice which changes theology along with the world. As a result we have not deduced the theology of revolution from Lehmann's outline, but have followed its construction among those who speak from actual practice. But this is only to confirm once again the common fundamental feature: to qualify the action of man not from his possibilities, even though they may be Christian, but from a divine context – and that means one that goes beyond the individual, that transcends the existing state of affairs in social and revolutionary terms. Seen in a wider context, the theology of revolution goes beyond at least the modern period of Protestant theology. This is also what it shares with many theological trends of the twentieth century, and explains why it has been accepted in so many areas.

These last remarks already show us the way towards a wider characterization of this theology. They mark its limits as a critical theology. The material weight of the social and political conflicts which this movement seeks to resolve is oppressive, and where the need for progress is so obvious, there is little ground for advancing qualifications and limitations. Nevertheless, the permanent success of a theology involved with these issues must be a matter for urgent debate. In theological structure, the critical progress made by the theology of revolution is in the last resort no more than a step towards an uncritical theology. We shall now take up the theme of its ambivalence from another aspect and make it more precise from three perspectives.

The theology of revolution is *political theology* and as such is theology which has so to speak been developed politologically. It brings into prominence the sociological and political conditioning of traditional theology and the church and draws consequences from this for its own construction. In effect, however, it is itself a *theology of the church* transformed into a theology of history, and consequently follows the laws of all ecclesiastical theologies, albeit in a novel way. That is, it binds to its communion all the good that can be conceived and realized in this or in a future world.

As political theology the theology of revolution is *public theology*. That is, it declares public questions such as those of community life and its political and social structure to be relevant to Christians, and allows theological interest to break out of the closed context of the individual search for salvation. The universality of the public realm is the critical medium of political reason. For the theological significance of the public realm, however, God stands as the higher authority of a justification of the criticism of Christian attitudes, an authority which is at the same time withdrawn from that critical medium of the public realm. This theology is therefore a *theology of revelation* turned towards the political realm. Granted, this gives permanence to the revolutionary impulse, but at the same time this theology can no longer be applied to concrete situations which are quite capable of change and which in particular instances may be an occasion for revolutionary action.

Finally, in accordance with its structural genesis, the theology of revolution displays the features of *Enlightenment theology*, a theology which is indebted to the critical heritage of the Enlightenment. Its power to enlighten can be seen both from the utilization of the arguments of the social sciences and sociology and in the transformation of the function of theological categories. But the Enlightenment serves it more as an arsenal of critical instruments; it does not take over the themes of Enlightenment, particularly when one remembers the intentions of Christian Enlightenment theology. In effect, it tends towards a *left-wing orthodoxy*, if one may be permitted to use this not unknown simile from modern history. For it achieves its consistency in a presentation of material which is in place in the pre-critical and above all the biblical realm, and takes its stand in a world which is no longer that of the Enlightenment and its consequences; so it is revolutionary orthodoxy.

Finally, its *tendency towards irrationality* is unmistakable. In favour of this one could argue that it is the result of social conditions which have become irrational because they are no longer comprehensible and cannot be expressed in categories of action. In addition it could be associated with the demand that society's own rationality, which has become *repressive*, must be burst asunder. This question, which occupies any analysis of our time and of society, cannot be discussed on its own here. But at this point Enlightenment is topical today at that very point where the limitations of an all-embracing, even theological interpretation of the world are experienced and therefore everything tends to move towards action which will change such a situation. The ecumenical consciousness today tends towards such irrationalism in the demand for action. Here a new form of immediacy comes into being which is not that of the individual subject to itself, expressed in existential categories, but an immediacy to the whole of society and history.

But is not Lehmann's formula *Ethics in a Christian Context* simply a reversal of that other formula, *Christian Faith in the Context of Ethics*, with which Christianity once achieved its progress into modern times? Cannot and must not action also be defined in a context – namely that of ethics – which is not the irrational total of reality and society, but which takes a productive view of the specific limits of man in his world? Is not the ethical consciousness which has become almost universal in the modern world the authority which shows the world where criticism is needed and where change is required? And does not a theology which seeks to bring God and the world and action into a series such as has been indicated here hold back ethics, hinder its consequences instead of furthering them? Is freedom only the characteristic of a future world or society? Or is it not the measure of our finite world, by which even theology must be measured, allowing itself to be bounded by ethics and no longer making promises about men's action? Questions about questions which also require answers. They arise on the boundaries of the theology of revolution.

Jürgen Moltmann · *God in Revolution*

Jürgen Moltmann, *Religion, Revolution and the Future*, Charles Scribner's Sons, NY 1969, pp.130-47. Reprinted by permission. © 1969 by Jürgen Moltmann

THESIS 1: *We live in a revolutionary situation. In the future we shall experience history more and more as revolution. We can be responsible for the future of man only in a revolutionary way.*

The threefold occurrence of the words 'revolution' and 'revolutionary' in this thesis seems a bit overdone. Since Vietnam and Cuba, and since the racial struggles in the United States and the student uprisings in Western and Eastern Europe, it has become a catchword and faded into a commonplace. And yet men are still not consciously geared to the new situation which the word 'revolution' denotes. Christians and the churches seem to find peculiar difficulty in engaging this new revolutionary situation ...

In the future we shall experience history more and more as revolution. What is 'revolution'? I understand revolution to mean a transformation in the foundations of a system – whether of economics, of politics, of morality, or of religion. All other changes amount to evolution or reform. But transformation in the foundations of a system becomes a genuine possibility only when previously unsuspected possibilities or powers are at hand. Only then does there emerge a critical consciousness in the present. We compare what is actual with what is possible and find a discrepancy between actuality and possibility. We realize that the future could be different from the present. We live today in a world of unrealized but quite realizable humanity. Now that it is really possible to eliminate hunger in the world and to control overpopulation, the systems which hinder the realization of these possibilities must be radically changed. Today real possibilities are flooding the existing institutions for realizing them. Hence, in the critical consciousness, the future as the fullness of possibilities comes into conflict with the constricting institutions of the present. And, by the same token, in the reactionary and repressive consciousness, the possession of the present comes into conflict with the new future ...

We are compelled to take responsibility for man's future in a revolutionary way. Involvement in a contemporary search for truth will mean discovering, as Gramsci did, that 'truth is revolutionary.' It will mean discovering that the world can be changed and that nothing has to remain as it has been. It will mean testing scientific theories by the imperative of transforming reality. The historical praxis which wants to realize a freer and more just humanity becomes the practical horizon of the development of theories. Scientific knowledge, then, is a means to the self-liberation of man from obdurate dependence only when it is employed in responsibility for a more humane future. To be responsible for history in a revolutionary fashion today means to find the unity of knowledge and action.

THESIS 2: *The new revolutionary situation has brought Christianity into a deep crisis of identity. Christians and the churches will rediscover their true self-consciousness only if they overcome their own religious alienation and their own hindrance to the free self-realization of man.*

'There is no theology of revolution,' say our solicitous bishops. And they are right. For the theology of revolution is certainly no theology for bishops, but a lay theology of Christians who are suffering and struggling in the world. On the other hand, it must be said that there will be no 'theology of revolution' until there is a revolution in theology. As long as Christians refrain from acting in a revolutionary way, they have no right to make theological declarations about revolution. Neither does the church have a right to a 'theology of revolution' in the world if it is not engaged in its own radical transformation. It is totally inauthentic for the church to speak and act against the economic alienation of man without struggling against the spiritual alienation which it itself propagates. We cannot say very much about the 'new earth' as long as we do not realize that the heaven of religion has become old and repressive and that we need a 'new heaven.' 'The critique of heaven is being changed into a critique of earth, the critique of religion into a critique of law, the critique of theology into a critique of politics,' said Karl Marx. Today it is just the reverse ...

It is the hope of committed Christians that the church can change. They are aware of the deep discrepancy between the hitherto realized form of Christianity and its unrealized possibilities. They suffer because faith is bound to anxiety in the face of the future. They are frustrated by the repressive character of ecclesiastical morality. They are thwarted by the authoritarian structures of church polity and by clerical manipulation. They are searching for a faith which is free and united with hope in the face of the future. They demand the individual responsibility of man in the dimension of personal morality. After the church has for so long narrowly presented the heavenly Christ in Word, sacrament and hierarchy, they seek communion with the crucified Son of man who waits among the hungry, the naked, the prisoner, and the refugee for the acts of righteousness.

THESIS 3: *The eschatological (and messianic) tradition of hope can give rise to a new birth of Christian faith in the revolutionary present.*

Christians are known as 'those who have a hope' (Eph. 2:12; 1 Thess. 4:13). In the crucified Proclaimer of the kingdom of freedom they see the old world crucified and the new world revealed. Therefore they lift themselves up out of humiliation by other men and out of resignation to fate in order to proclaim the coming God and his Christ, who will bring to an end the suffering of the whole creation. In the sacral-political world of antiquity, these Christians acted as revolutionaries of both heaven and earth. They scorned the so-called gods of the fatherland and refused to sacrifice to the Roman emperor-god. They were not satisfied with *Pax Romana* but eagerly waited for *Pax Christi*. Celsus, the famous second-century critic of Christianity, reproached Christians for causing a 'tumult' (*stasis*) in heaven by refraining from sacrifice to the gods. This rebellious stubborness has serious consequences to the anger of the gods. But as revolutionaries of heaven they simultaneously inflict the religio-political order on earth with confusion. They are therefore public enemies of the state and traitors to humanity. Neither Paul nor the early Christian theologians developed a 'theology of revolution.' Yet through their worship of God in the crucified Jesus, the Christians were certainly acting as revolutionaries. For by so doing they seized the nerve-centre of the political religions and the religious politics of their time. Their theology was a revolution at that time even though they had no 'theology of revolution' ...

This stream of eschatological messianism may be generally represented by the word 'new.' The prophets proclaimed to the Hebrews in exile and captivity a 'new exodus,' a 'new occupation of the Promised Land,' a 'new Zion' and a 'new Jerusalem,' and even a 'new David.' They blended into the message of the new future of Israel the as-yet-never-existing reality of a greater future: ultimate salvation and universal redemption for the whole creation. In the New Testament the apostles proclaim the 'new man,' the 'new covenant,' the 'new song,' the 'new wine,' the 'new people of God' and in the end 'the new creation of heaven and earth.' This universal Christian message of the new is manifestly anchored in the expectation of the God who in the end says: 'Behold, I make all things new.'

The new future in this tradition enters into transitory history, as it were, in waves of anticipation. It appears first in the mission of the Christ of God, who personally incarnates the future of freedom among the unfree and in his resurrection opens up the future to everything which is dying. Then in the mission of the gospel's words of the future the sinner is forgiven, the Godless justified, and the humiliated given hope. Then the new future comes in the mission of the community of Christ, which, as the 'new people of God' drawn from all nations and tongues, is the vanguard of the new humanity and the representative embodiment of freedom from the coercive powers of this world. Then it arrives in the new obedience of the believers, who in ordinary life refuse to conform to the scheme of this world, but anticipate the coming freedom. Finally, it comes in the 'new heaven and the new earth' where justice dwells, where Christ's presence purges heaven of religious myths and powers and frees the earth from pain, sorrow, and meaningless death . . .

THESIS 4: *The new criterion of theology and of faith is to be found in praxis.*

The aim of Marx's critique of religion was the categorical imperative 'to overthrow all circumstances in which man is a humiliated, an enslaved, a forsaken and a despised being.' Not only for him, but for the whole modern age, ethical and political praxis has become the test of theories. Truth must be practicable. Unless it contains initiative for the transformation of the world, it becomes a myth of the existing world. Because reality has become historical and man experiences himself as a historical being, he will find a possible conformity of consciousness and existence only in historical praxis. This is the event of truth.

The Christian tradition of hope in the coming God and the new creation has not always adhered to this criterion of truth. Even the Christian future hope was frequently speculative and narrated the events of the last times as if they were past history. But only the past can be narrated; the future has to be historically anticipated in word and deed. The Christian hope was also frequently merely consolation in the afterlife which God would guarantee. In this capacity, it served to unnerve historical life. But, on the other hand, we should not forget that eschatological visions were originally the visions of the Christian martyrs on their way into exile or the arena and thus related quite well to the practice of martyrdom. The critical question was framed by Walter Rauschenbusch: 'Ascetic Christianity called the world evil and left it. Humanity is waiting for a revolutionary Christianity which will call the world evil and change it.' Under the conditions of modern times, the eschatological symbolism of Christian hope appears to be mythical. But it dare not dream away any longer about an eternity beyond time. It must bring the hoped-for future into practical contact with the misery of the present. This is necessary not only on the basis of the modern historical world; it is also a demand of Jesus himself. He not merely announced the Kingdom of God, but practised it in his love of sinners and publicans ...

For Christian hope the world is not an insignificant waiting room for the soul's journey to heaven, but the 'arena' of the new creation of all things and the battleground of freedom. Christian hope dare not evacuate the present by dreaming about the future; nor may it compensate for an empty present by dreaming about the future. It must, rather, draw the hoped-for future already into the misery of the present and use it in practical initiatives for overcoming this misery. Through criticism and protest, on the one hand, and creative imagination and action, on the other, we can avail ourselves of freedom for the future.

Because the practice of the church is the strongest weapon of criticism of the church today, Christians will be judged by whether they live the truth of Jesus and verify their faith practically.

THESIS 5: *The church is not a heavenly arbiter in the world's strifes. In the present struggles for freedom and justice, Christians must side with the humanity of the oppressed.*

The church is for all men, say some. Therefore, it should remain strictly separated from political struggle. Since there are no unequivocal Christian judgments in politics, the church should religiously be in the service of all sides. This is the old ecclesiastical triumphalism in modern dress as offered by the representatives of organized churches to the contending parties. Here the church is always 'the third power,' a 'neutral platform' for peace and reconciliation, a 'place for meeting' and negotiating. *Sub specie aeternitatis* all worldly conflicts become relative and insignificant. There was a time when this mediating role of the church was occasionally in demand and was instrumental in promoting tranquillity. But today all ambiguous and abstract appeals for peace fall on deaf ears, as was demonstrated in the speech of Pope Paul VI to the United Nations. Struggling factions have become tired of appeals to their conscience and of verbose sermons on morality. They do not expect from the church any transcendent wisdom to aid the resolution of their conflicts.

Yet, if Christians take sides in the political struggle, will they not lose sight of God's love for all men? This is the question from the other point of view. I do not think that they need to lose it. The goal of Christian universalism can be realized precisely through the dialectic of siding with the humiliated ... By undermining and demolishing all barriers – whether of religion, race, education, or class – the community of Christians proves that it is the community of Christ. This could indeed become the new identifying mark of the church in our world, that it is composed, not of equal and like-minded men, but of dissimilar men, indeed even of former enemies. This would mean, on the other hand, that national churches, class churches, and race churches are false churches of Christ and already heretical as a result of their concrete struture ...

Albert Camus described the humane principle of revolution in this way: The slave revolts against his master. He denies him as a master, but not as a man. For his protest is directed against the master's refusal to treat him as a man. As master and slave, neither is a true man and neither can relate to the other in a humane way. If the denial of the master were total, the slave's revolt would bring nothing new into the world but would only exchange the roles of inhumanity. The humane revolution, however, is not out to turn the slaves into masters but to subvert and abolish the whole master-slave relationship so that in the future men will be able to treat one another as men. If the revolution loses sight of this goal, it becomes nihilistic and forfeits its fascination.

In this sense, Christianity's taking sides with the 'damned of the earth' is a way to the redemption and reconciliation of the damned and the damners. Only through the dialectic of taking sides can the universalism of salvation make its entrance into the world. Any ecclesiastical triumphalism is, therefore, an immature anticipation of the Kingdom of God.

THESIS 6 : *The problem of violence and nonviolence is an illusory problem. There is only the question of the justified and unjustified use of force and the question of whether the means are proportionate to the ends.*

Those who advocate nonviolence today are usually those who control the police power. Those who embrace revolutionary violence are usually those who have no means of power. This is a paradox. It is fully clear that the transformation of the conditions of power will come only through the use of power and the assumption of authority. The sole problem consists of the fact that power must be justified; else it is nothing but 'naked violence.' The use of revolutionary violence must be justified by the humane goals of the revolution and the existing power structures unmasked in their inhumanity as 'naked violence.' Otherwise, revolutionary violence cannot be made meaningful or appropriate. Unless every possible means is put to use, the revolutionary future is not worth committing oneself to, but if disproportionate means are employed, then the goals of the revolution are betrayed ...

Only with great restraint can revolutionaries enter the *diabolical circle* of violence and counterviolence if they are ever to conquer and abolish it as a whole. Revolutionary means must constantly be reconciled with humane goals, else the revolution threatens to end in terrorism and resignation. How are we to bring about the kingdom of nonviolent brotherhood with the help of violent actions? This is the inner aporia of revolutionary activity. Those who allow the law of the opposition to prescribe their own course are, in any case, not yet the new humanity. Any means may be appropriate, but they must be different and better than those of the opposition if they are to bewilder the opposition. Martin Luther King, Jr., spoke and acted from out of a dimension of truth which was not dependent on political power and the rules of its game. He was to a great extent immune against the anxiety and seduction of power. And precisely for that reason he became more threatening than the prophets of violence to those in positions of power ...

THESIS 7: *The presence of Christians in revolutions can mean that revolutions are freed from the coercion of the law.*

Only with some circumspection and much self-criticism do I venture this last thesis. It is not meant *pedantically* but, rather, expresses a hope. Revolutions have a tendency towards legalism. In an understandable but also regrettable way, they are often dominated by a moralism by which they view themselves as good and the opposition as inevitably bad. They are of course right to criticize the evil of the opposition. This moralism awakens a new self-affirmation in their own camp as well as a previously unknown sense of solidarity with the comrades in arms; it is only right to appreciate these new-found values. But seldom is there much sensitivity for the ambiguity in even the the best of human lives. To be sure, there may be a developed self-criticism in face of one's own mistakes. But this self-criticism does not prevent the

Stalinistic fallacy of one's own achievements. Revolutionaries often resemble the old Puritans who took themselves with 'deep seriousness' and forgot how to laugh at themselves. This is all quite understandable and perhaps even inevitable.

But I would expect from Christians, who believe in God's presence in the midst of revolution, that they would laugh and sing and dance as the first to be liberated in creation ... The spirit of the final world revolution comes to life in every historical revolution. World-transforming love is sustained by world-surpassing hope. I think that in this way Christian faith can free man from the convulsions of anxiety and vengeance. I believe that at this point the deep earnestness of love for suffering man can be joined with the cheerful play of faith in God. To faith's practical initiatives for the world's future belongs also something like the mysticism of joy in the present God.

The Christian God is no heavenly guarantor of the status quo. But neither is he the avenging God of the offended. In him is found that eternal joy which causes the whole creation to sing and dance. Marxism speaks of the transformation of work into free spontaneity. This is the transition from the 'kingdom of necessity' into the 'kingdom of freedom.' This idea has a long history and is also alive in Christianity. [Here it means the liberation from the law of works by faith, which brings forth the free fruits of love.] In mysticism it is the idea of the transformation of labour conditioned by need into the play of freedom. Labour conditioned by need or by self-assertion is labour which alienates and humiliates man. Revolutionary work for another future of man is always dependent on what it wants to change and establish. What does faith mean other than already here and now in the midst of the kingdom of poverty and necessity to begin realizing the future of freedom, love, and play? Where this spirit of freedom reigns, of freedom not only from masters and exploiters, but also freedom of man from himself, where this spirit of festivity and laughing becomes infectious, there the revolution within the revolution can take place, the deliverance of revolution from the alienating forms which it assumes in the struggle. It was a student in Tübingen who transformed the saying of Che Guevara: 'The vocation of every lover is to bring about revolution' into 'The duty of every revolution is to bring about love.'

Harvey Cox · *Anatomy of a Revolutionary Theology*

Harvey Cox, *The Secular City*, SCM Press, London and Macmillan Co., NY 1965; revised edition, Macmillan Co. 1966 and Penguin Books, London 1968, pp.125-32, 134. Reprinted by permission. © Harvey Cox, 1965, 1966

Does the coming of the secular city provide us with the necessary basis for a theology of revolution?

Any workable revolutionary theory must exhibit four essential features. It must include (1) a notion of why action is now necessary, and this notion must be capable of catalysing action; therefore we call this first ingredient that *catalytic*. It must include (2) an explanation of why some people have *not* acted so far and still refuse to act, an interpretation of their inability to see or to move. Webster defines catalepsy as a mental disease characterized by rigidity and inability to move. What we see here is a kind of social catalepsy, a political paralysis; hence we call this second feature of an adequate revolutionary theory its *interpretation of catalepsy*. But the theory must also have (3) a view on how people can be changed, how they can be brought out of their cataleptic stupor and encouraged to act. It must have an *idea of catharsis*, the purgative process by which the hindrances to action are eliminated. Since this purgation always occurs by means of a radical alteration of the environment of the social cataleptic, every revolutionary theory must have it, and (4) finally, an *understanding of catastrophe* – again according to Webster, 'an event overturning the order or system of things'. It is the catastrophe, the social denouement, which makes possible a change in those who are unable to move and thereby facilitates purposeful action.

The catalytic factor in most revolutionary theories appears in the form of what might be called a *catalytic gap*, the idea that a lag exists which must now be closed, and that closing it is the action required. Awareness of the gap provides the catalytic agent which releases change. In most revolutionary theories, this catalytic gap is viewed as a lag between one aspect of civilization and another. Thus for the French *philosophes*, the Age of Reason had already dawned among thinking people, but the priests and princes were still purveying superstitious absurdities. For the Russian Bolsheviks, the dialectic of history had opened the door to a classless society while both the tsars and their ineffectual social-democratic successors still dawdled in the vestibule. Both theories provided a potent source of accelerated social change.

Today the catalytic gap suggested by the theorists of the French and Russian revolutions no longer fills the bill. In fact, we lack any potent revolutionary theory. Scientific technology and medical research have ushered us precipitately into a civilization for which neither our political nor our cultural institutions are prepared. Though our predicament can be partially illuminated by Marx's diagnosis of the economic substructure outrunning the political superstructure, in reality our dilemma is a vastly more complex one. We are entering an era in which power is based not on property but on technical knowledge and intellectual skills. We are rushing headlong from the production line to the linear computer, from work to leisure values, from an industrial to an automated society – and our political processes as well as our cultural and religious symbols still reflect the bygone pre-technical society. Our infant republic has sprouted and shot up in every direction, and we can no longer button its clothes around it. We are still trying to dress a rapidly growing technological society in political rompers. This lag should have provided us with the catalytic gap we need, but so far it has not. Our accumulating crises in mass transit, housing, and growing unemployment dramatize our inability to deal politically with the problems created by technological change. We need a new revolutionary theory, pertinent to the pressures of the times.

This is why the word *technopolis* suggests both the possibilities and the problems of our new urban civilization. *Techno* symbolizes the technical base on which the secular city rests, *polis* recalls the social and cultural institutions without which the technical environment becomes an unliveable monstrosity. Together they suggest the tension out of which social change can emerge. We are now choking on a serious imbalance between the technical and the political components of technopolis. This should create our catalytic gap. The challenge we face confronts us with the necessity of weaving a political harness to steer and control our technical centaurs.

Again the biblical image of the Kingdom of God, transcribed for our times into the symbol of the secular city, the commonwealth of maturity and interdependence, provides a catalytic gap. God is always one step ahead of man. Man repeatedly encounters God in the Bible as the One who beckons him to come from where he is to a different place. Motion, from here to there and from now to then, fixes the crucial axis of the Bible. The Kingdom of God has never come in its fullness and perfection, so man can take his ease. Yet it is never so distant and unattainable that man can only surrender in despair. Rather, the Kingdom of God is always just arriving. It is always the 'coming Kingdom', the new reality which is beginning to appear. Its initial marks are always *becoming* visible.

The catalytic gap from the biblical viewpoint is provided by the semicolon in the phrase which is the very first sentence attributed to Jesus by the oldest Gospel, Mark: 'The time is fulfilled, and the kingdom of God is at hand; repent, and believe the Gospel!' (1:15). When this epochal announcement is utilized, as the community of faith does, not just to comprehend Jesus but also to illumine the whole of historic reality, we can see that man is placed in a permanent catalytic gap. The Apostle Paul caught the same mood when he summarized the life of faith with the following phrase: '... forgetting what lies behind and straining forward to what lies ahead, I press on towards the goal ...' (Philippians 3:13). The Bible places this present age in the crevasse between what was and what will be. For this reason the ethical tension seen by the Bible is somewhat different from the tension between what is and what ought to be, as it is usually stated in philosophical ethics. The grammar of the Gospel is not a categorical imperative; it first of all points to what *is* occurring, only secondarily does it call for a consequent change in attitude and action. The Kingdom of God is at hand; therefore repent.

The syntax of the secular city is identical. Through its irrepressible emergence it establishes a new situation which renders former ways of thinking and doing wholly obsolete. When called to man's attention, secularization summons him to action. It creates its own gap, catalysing man to close it if he wishes to remain man and not be overwhelmed by the forces of history.

Then why does man *not* act? When the ancient imagery of a kingdom is translated into contemporary idiom, why does he still turn away? Even when he hears the Gospel as a summons to leave behind the society and symbols of a dying era and to assume responsibility for devising new ones, why does he refuse? Here we need to explore the *social catalepsis*, the blindness and paralysis which prevent men from acting to close the gap.

Theologians have insisted that man always remains capable of saying no to the Gospel, if he wishes to. He may cling tenaciously to the patterns and purposes of a previous era the way insecure children sometimes continue to clutch to themselves a blanket or bib that comforted them in infancy, but this refusal clearly represents a flight from maturity. It condemns a man to live in what the New Testament calls 'this dying age'. It will result in an increasing disorientation and a growing sense of unreality. This in turn will produce mountingly frantic and ultimately fruitless efforts to grasp the import of events in terms that are no longer adequate.

But the question remains, Why do people who are caught in the catalytic gap still stalwartly refuse to change? The Marxists' answer to the problem of social catalepsy remains a classic one. They explain it with their notion of 'false consciousness'. They suggest that consciousness itself springs from a social matrix, in particular from one's relationship to the means of production. Therefore a person whose ties to property place him within the patterns of the passing era has his view of the world poisoned, so to speak. He perceives things wrongly. Though he is caught in the hiatus between past and future, he cannot change because he cannot *see* that he is caught. The only way to change his viewpoint is to change the point from which the view originates; this means to separate him from his property. As we shall notice when we discuss the Marxist catharsis, depriving a man of his property is really a liberation. It releases him from his interest in a society marked for destruction and thus acts as an antidote to the poison that contaminates his vision. Logically, the total abolition of all private property cures everyone of this social trachoma and all false consciousness disappears.

Biblical thought also delves into the dilemma of why men do not respond to the coming of the Kingdom. Men are 'sinners'; they suffer from a deformed and distorted vision of themselves, society, and reality as a whole. The sinner is infirm. His sickness festers into a fatal incapacity to see or hear properly what is going on in his environment. Hence he is in the middle of the catalytic gap but does not know it. He is like a person living in a trance induced by posthypnotic suggestion. The Bible describes this condition with a wide variety of figures, including lameness, deafness, sleep, and death. Paul suggests that persons in this condition have been mesmerized. In scolding the backsliders of Galatia he pointedly asks them who has bewitched (hypnotized) them. In other places such people are described as being in chains, in prison, in darkness. The similes combine to depict a condition in which the person is unable to see his world clearly or to respond to it appropriately. He has a jaundiced view of reality and his capacity to react is crippled. This is why when Paul writes to the early Christians he often tells them to 'wake up!' – to snap out of their trance. When the followers of John the Baptist come to Jesus and ask him point-blank if he is the promised one or should they wait for another, he replies, significantly, by telling them to look around them at what is happening: the blind see, the deaf hear, the lame walk, and the poor have the Gospel preached to them.

But now comes the problems of *catharsis*. What caused these people to wake up from their stupor, to see what they had been missing before? The process is called in the New Testament *metanoia*, a very radical change. The former self dies and a new self is born. It is a total change for the person involved: '... all things become new.' No one is seen any more from simply a human point of view. It is like being 'born again' or coming alive from the dead. It is conversion, a sweeping change in one's perception of self and world. It results in a life in which one is now able to see, hear, walk, and leap for joy. Obstacles to perception and to response are both removed. Man can now see what is happening in his world and react appropriately.

Another important group of New Testament images for conversion, or the transformation of one's perception of reality, are those denoting the achievement of maturity, coming of age and adulthood. 'When I became a man,' says Saint Paul, 'I put away childish things.' In the letter to the Galatians he compares the man of faith with a person who has been under the governance of a tutor during his minority but now attains the age of accountability and becomes a full heir to his father's estate. As heir the son must now bear full responsibility for the administration of the estate.

These images of maturity and responsibility are crucial for our argument here since secularization itself can be viewed as a process of maturing and assuming responsibility. Secularization signifies the removal of religious and metaphysical supports and putting man on his own. It is unlocking the gate of the playpen and turning man loose in an open universe. Consequently it is important to notice that maturation and responsibility symbols are in no sense exceptional in the New Testament. They appear for instance in several of the parables attributed to Jesus in which he speaks of stewards who are given charge of an estate while the master goes away. Their assignment includes not just the care of sums of money for which they will be held accountable. It includes also a responsibility for the mature and judicious treatment of the master's servants. Thus the drunken steward who beats the servants is judged with great severity. He has betrayed an assignment, the stewardship of power. Entirely too much has been said in most churches about the stewardship of money and too little about the stewardship of power. The modern equivalent of repentance is the responsible use of power.

But what brings about the catharsis? What causes man to

change, to repent, to revolt, to accept responsibility for power? A revolutionary theology, like a revolutionary theory, must make a place for catastrophe, in the technical sense of an event which overturns the order of things.

For Marx the catastrophe was the objective condition growing out of the development of industrialization which placed the power in the hands of the workers. Revolutionary action merely brought the political superstructure in line with the existing reality of the substructure. Though Marx may seem to dodge on the issue, his view of revolution is a clear example of man's doing something and his having something happen to him all at once. The revolution is no more paradoxical than the Incarnation.

For Marx, this catastrophe, this overturning, provide the essential prerequisite for catharsis. He saw that an objective condition, the removal of their property, was the indispensable precondition for correcting the false consciousness of capitalists. This is why Marx was so impatient with intellectuals who wanted to argue or persuade people out of their political ideas or religious beliefs. People's opinions, Marx believed, could only be changed by altering the social reality on which they were based. He was tired of those philosophers who had spent their lives interpreting the world. 'The time has come', he said, 'to change it.'

Similarly, for the Bible the coming of the new order of the Kingdom is the catastrophe. It provides the indispensable precondition for waking up. Paul never believed that just a shout from him would wake up the entranced Galatians. What enabled them to slough off their sleep was the new reality in which they had been placed by God's action in Christ. Paul's words had power only because they were uttered in the context of the Kingdom, which he referred to more often as the New Creation or the new era.

Our perception of reality is highly conditioned. It is influenced by our personal careers, our social location, the job we hold, and the web of meanings arising from all of these by which the ideas and experiences we encounter are screened and selected. Hence our perceptions of reality can be changed only as these conditions themselves are changed.

This is an immensely important fact for any theology of social change, any revolutionary theology, to take into consideration. It implies that people simply cannot be expected to see or react responsibly to emerging social and political problems merely by hearing sermons or reading articles. Something else has to change first. The summons they hear must occur within the matrix of a new social situation, a new objective context which provides the basis for a changed perception of reality. The catastrophe precedes the catharsis. The Kingdom of God precedes repentance ...

Catastrophe and catharsis come again and again. Just as the Bible sees God's Kingdom coming to man time and again, demanding a new response each time, so in our terms the secularization of history keeps going on. The human world is never fully humanized; therefore, again and again we must 'cast off the works of darkness.' We must be ready to react to new realities in history by discarding even our most cherished ideas and accepting new ones, later to be sacrificed again. 'We are always *becoming* Christians,' observed Kierkegaard wisely. We are always becoming mature and responsible stewards. Permanent revolution requires permanent conversion.

4 · Theology of Development

Even in 1968 it was clear that Europe was incapable of transforming itself from within. 'Revolution' was the only word that could be used to describe the dimensions of qualitative change required to move from the present to the new future of man. But in the ears of most Europeans 'revolution' does not stimulate action but brings about a certain fearful paralysis. Yet if Europe was incapable of bringing about such change by itself a new configuration had appeared, a new factor with which to reckon. Europe certainly did not dominate the world, nor even the West and the East taken together, for now the Third World had emerged both in frustration and impatience. It could not be ignored, either in economic terms or in ideological terms. We shall mention both of these areas.

More dramatic than any political division of the world is the economic division which places the USA and the USSR firmly on the same side of a line and over against the majority of people in the world. As early as the founding of the UN the disparity of developed and underdeveloped countries was pointed out. However, the disparity does not refer simply to the internal development of nations. Development in some countries has brought about the power to control others and to draw on their resources. The division between developed and underdeveloped is also one of powerful and weak, rich and poor and more ominously a division of white north against black south.

The disparity may have originally derived from a historical accident but it is not perpetuated by chance. The gap between the two groups is actually widening. The initial development of the poor countries has only brought more serious problems. Control of endemic disease has led to a vast increase in population. The aid given from the rich nations has meant crippling sums to be repaid from an economy which is little better off than at the beginning of the development programme. The result has led to a decrease generally in the standard of living in the poor countries at a time when an increase is experienced in the rich. This fact of experience is often disguised by the way in which the GNP in poor countries often must exclude reference to subsistence farming.

The kind of development that has taken place has tended to serve the rich nations better than the poor. For example it often leads to the development of a single crop economy geared to provide raw materials for the industries of the north. The mineral wealth of these countries tends to be exploited long before it can be used within the poor country. Capital intensive development has provided relatively little employment for local people. Even when foreign companies are set up in the south profits are withdrawn – sometimes in hard currency.

Political independence has not altered the economic facts inherited by the new leaders. Even in extreme cases where they nationalize the assets of the northern companies the trade patterns remain, unfavourable terms persist and they still supply raw materials for northern development. It is therefore misleading to think that north and south are at different stages in a world-wide process of development. The poor nations are not like small trees planted later than the now grown trees. The relationship is more complex than that. The widening of the gap should draw our attention to the fact that we are not dealing with two groups at different stages in a single development process. There is indeed one process, and it is a process by which development in the north takes place at the expense of development in the south. Given the disparity it is not true to say that trade benefits everyone. The terms of trade are controlled by one side. It has been made abundantly clear at successive UNCTAD conferences that the north has no intention of changing these terms and so altering the relationship of rich and poor. For this reason development has become a moral and even theological issue.

The 1950s saw a period of hope and rising expectations among the poor countries: the 1960s were years of disillusionment. If development had been allowed to take place in the Third World then the countries of the south would have fallen in behind those of the north, following the models and patterns of development already established in the rich countries. The fact that economically and politically this path was closed enabled the people of the south to consider a more fundamental issue, namely whether they should so uncritically assume that the model of the rich countries was the model for the whole world. At this point also the development debate raises moral and theological issues. Assuming that 'development' is good are there different kinds of development? Is economic development the sole or most important criterion of development? Should affluence be the goal of development? Is human life fully developed when it is characterized by wealth of possessions and a high level of consumption?

If economic relations gave rise to a moral criticism of the north, the failure of development gave rise to a further criticism about the north's understanding of man and society. At the early stage in the world concern for development it was assumed that the rich nations possessed that to which the poor should aspire. Value flowed in one direction. Now we see a counter flow, in which while the south would dearly love to end its poverty the example of the north is no longer automatically accepted as normative. Once again Frantz Fanon has been influential. Fanon was born in Martinique and studied medicine in France. He came to see that he had been processed in such a way as to become a European and therefore, in spite of his black skin, to be acceptable to whites. This was a concrete example of the one-way flow of values by which the Third World was maintained in an inferior position to the West. In *The Wretched of the Earth* he consciously turns his back on the West and addresses himself to the Third World. 'Let us try to create the whole man, whom Europe has been incapable of bringing to triumphant birth.' When the former colonies become independent, how are they to use their freedom? Are they immediately to turn in behind their former masters and perpetuate the old relationships? This would simply confirm the values of Europe, the very values which colonized and created under-development. For the sake of the Third World a new way must be found. Indeed the hope of Europe lies in the Third World finding a new way. 'Moreover, if we wish to reply to the expectations of the people of Europe, it is no good sending them back a reflection, even an ideal reflection, of their society and their thought with which from time to time they feel immeasurably sickened. For Europe, for ourselves and for humanity, comrades, we must turn over a new leaf, we must work out new concepts and try to set afoot the new man.'

And so the development debate became a debate about man. More than that, while Europe looked to its former colonies and urged that contact be maintained (for the sake of Europe's future and affluence) Fanon called for contacts to be maintained for the sake of Europe's humanity. While Europe spoke of colonialism and economic advantage, Fanon spoke of decolonialization and the creation of the new man. Once again the neo-Marxist was more

confident than many European Christians that man does not live by
bread alone – and need not aspire to cake.

Revolution had tried to deal with qualitative change: development seemed a more comprehensive way of dealing with the issue,
at least when development was about humanization. 'Theology of
revolution' had always seemed improbable in Europe and so
political theology became better expressed as theology of development. All the fundamental issues about man's present and future
were already gathered up in the development debate. Theologians
simply had to make a Christian contribution to the debate about
man, society and the use of the world's resources. A long neglected
side of the good news came to be mentioned increasingly: 'I came
that they may have life, and have it abundantly.'

Church leaders often lack credibility when speaking of revolution and seldom seem at ease with the subject. But development
was different and the theology of development was taken up with
enthusiasm in places where theology of revolution had been
shunned. (The acceptability of the idea of development had its own
significance, and to this we shall return in the next chapter.) The
World Council of Churches was early into the development debate,
investigating its moral and theological implications. This concern
can be seen in the conference in Geneva in 1966 on 'Church and
Society', the report of which was entitled *Christians in the Technical
and Social Revolution of our Time*. This was followed in March
1968 by the Zagorsk Consultation, near Moscow, on 'Theological
Issues of Church and Society'. The Third Section of the *Uppsala
Report* is on 'World Economic and Social Development'.

But perhaps the most significant fact in the emergent theology
of development was that it represented a concern also of the
Catholic Church, so that reflection on this issue became the basis
of a new kind of ecumenical theology. It was not, as so often in
the past, a discussion about matters internal to the churches. It
was an ecumenical response to an issue raised *for* the churches.
And since the world 'ecumenical' originally referred to the whole
inhabited world, then theology of development was doubly
ecumenical, since it was a concern of all the churches with a matter
affecting the whole world.

Concern with development can be traced to the work of J. L.
Lebret and appears in various forms in the 1950s, but it is with
Gaudium et Spes, and the *Pastoral Constitution on the Church in the
World Today* at the final session of the Council that the problem
of development was most explicitly raised. It was taken further by
the encyclical of Pope Paul in March 1967, *Populorum Progressio*

(ET 'On the Development of Peoples). Most significant of all was the setting up, at the beginning of 1968, of a body jointly by the Pontifical Commission for Justice and Peace and World Council of Churches. For the next three years this Committee on Society, Development and Peace (SODEPAX) produced very interesting and creative work and stimulated a good deal of practical activity in development programmes and projects.

Paul Löffler · *The Sources of a Christian Theology of Development*

Paul Löffler, 'The Sources of a Christian Theology of Development', *In search of a Theology of Development*, A SODEPAX Report, WCC, Geneva 1969, pp.65-73

A. ASSUMPTIONS

The approach taken in this paper assumes that:

1. The world-wide process of development represents a radically new situation for mankind in which there are at stake not only the relationship between rich and poor nations and thus the future of the world community, but also man's total human development, his liberation or alienation, and the shape of his whole society. In such a situation a mere adaptation of traditional theological positions will not do.

2. A double task of theological reflection has to be pursued. We need a contemporary articulation of faith interpreting theologically the new phenomena, a prophetic comment exposing the theological content of what is happening to men and by men. The other, perhaps less exciting, task is to establish connections between the issues posed by 'development' and the main strands of historic Christian thinking, i.e. to search out the record of faith found in the biblical canon and in the teaching of the churches for guidance towards the future and to check critically new insights in the light of the experience of the people of God throughout history. Only a dialectical interaction between the two exercises can result in an adequate theological perception of the processes of development.

Within the framework of the latter task the specific and limited objective of this paper is to indicate sources for theological study as found in biblical literature and interpreted in the teaching tradition of the Church as well as in the current theological discussions.

In order to find criteria for the selection of such sources and in order to establish focal points from which depth study can be launched, we need first to identify the main theological issues raised by development.

B. THEOLOGICAL ISSUES

The principal theological issues raised by the current development discussion are centred on the following three questions:
1. What is the motivation for development?
2. What are its goals?
3. Which methods should be used in implementing the goals?

1. *Motivation for development*

'Motivation' is understood here in two ways – as 'ideological presuppositions' which determine the policies of nations towards development, and as moral, economic, and political reasons which motivate individuals or groups such as Christian communities to participate in development. The second is a more obvious concern, but it must not blind us to the fact that no church can break out of the framework of ideology and politics of the respective nation for which it in turn shares responsibility. Both aspects of motivation raise theological issues:

(a) What is the prophetic ministry of the Church in unmasking political hypocrisy and ideological fallacy? How can Christians carry out this ministry, in particular vis-à-vis the political power structures and the mass media which influence the public stance and actual decisions concerning development? What are the main positive leads which could be given to influence a proper motivation of development?

(b) What is the significance of 'the unity of mankind'? The interdependence of peoples in the modern world and their responsibility for each other is being widely affirmed, not least by important ecumenical statements. Here lies one of the most fundamental and elementary motives for Christian participation in development. Yet several aspects obviously require further exploration:

(i) How does the emphasis on 'one human race' relate to the other biblical statements referring to different nations with their own historical and cultural identity, with differences in fate and conditions?

(ii) Assuming a pluralistic understanding of 'the unity of mankind', how do we deal with conflicts between the interests and goals within 'the family of nations', between the common good (who defines that?) and sectional interests?

(c) What are the possibilities and limitations of the creation mandate given to man?

(i) Already much has been said to emphasize the creation mandate given to man to master nature and to control his social environment. These statements need to be drawn together and compared. They will give a strong impetus to participation in development.

(ii) However, that emphasis has not been sufficiently connected with another strand of theological teaching: the meaning of suffering, the reality of death, the inability to fulfil the divine mandate. What is the bearing of these two dialectically opposed insights into the nature of man upon each other?

(d) What are the implications of the Christian understanding of 'justice' in a pluralistic society? The standard reference in Christian statements on development is to the strong biblical affirmation of social justice as found in particular in the Old Testament prophetic message and in the preaching of Christ. But there remain basic hermeneutical questions concerning the application of these passages to development in a pluralistically organized society today (see under Section D), and also questions of content:

(i) How does social, political, and economic justice relate to the theological concept of righteousness?

(ii) What are the criteria for translating the biblical directives into a different social context, from a situation assuming harmonious values into one of conflicting values?

2. *Goals for development*

By 'goals' I mean the aims and objectives, short-, medium-, and long-range, which determine the use of resources for development. They raise the following theological questions:

(a) Is it theologically possible to distinguish between short-, medium-, and long-range goals, and if so, what is their respective theological significance?

(b) Does the Christian understanding of creation, as interpreted by the social message of the Old Testament prophets and deepened through the incarnation of Christ, provide a frame for setting goals for development, and if so, what are its main outlines?

(c) The concept of a 'responsible society' has served as a main focus in ecumenical discussion since the 1930s. This concept has come under severe critique by those who feel that it is no longer dynamic enough for the revolutionary situation in many parts of the world. How can this be modified in order to provide a focal point capable of inspiring Christian involvement and giving it direction?

(d) 'Integral human development' or correspondingly 'humanization' have become the new watchwords. Both indicate vital problems in development which have nowhere been solved either in technologically developed or in developing societies. What guidelines do we receive for understanding human development from the study of Christ as the new man and from analysing patterns for a new humanity revealed in the design of the Church? How can the forces of alienation which engulf modern man be checked by the power of the Cross and Resurrection?

(e) What is in particular the tension and inter-relation between personal development through individual renewal and the development of the total community? Assuming an increasing conflict between individuals, groups, and institutions (structures), the theological discussion must give urgent attention to this dilemma.

(f) 'Continuity' versus 'change' is another inescapable tension in development. The issue is one of identity and security in the midst of rapid change as well as one of priorities of values and of goals. Can we draw up a scale of religious, cultural, and moral values which should be preserved according to Christian experience and tradition, in relation to the 'price' which will have to be paid in delay or limitation of development? What support does man need in order to live through rapid social change without losing his humanity?

3. *Methods of development*

By 'methods' I mean all instruments, ways, and means by which the goals of development are implemented. Methods raise another set of theological questions:

(a) Above all they raise the question of a Christian approach to the use of power:

(i) What is the Christian comment in the debate between those who demand the priority of revolutionary progress and those who are for reform and gradual evolution?

(ii) What are the generally applicable criteria to identify use and misuse of power in terms of its goals or in terms of unalienable human rights?

(iii) What is the pastoral responsibility towards those who feel compelled by their conscience to participate in violent revolution?

(iv) The Church as an organized group in society and as an institution exercises power (even where it is in a minority situation). In what way should it use its power, e.g. as a 'neutral pressure group' for good or as an ally of the poor and powerless?

(b) How can the Church be the Church in development? Roman Catholic pronouncements in particular have already stressed the ecclesiological elements in the discussion of development. Several aspects appear:

(i) The Church is called to be the beginning of the new humanity in this time and world. Further study is needed to indicate the *notae ecclesiae ad extram*, the signs which express the *pars pro toto* nature of the church vis-à-vis the new humanity.

(ii) In Christ as the head of the body, there are given standards of servanthood, self-giving, and sacrifice which the Church must follow. Further study is needed to determine the stance of service for the Church as a 'fellowship' as well as an institution which transcends national interests and contains within its membership rich and poor.

(iii) What are the responsibilities of and limitations for the Church's involvement in tackling the roots of social problems in society ('social diaconia')? How does the Church as a social institution relate to other social institutions (voluntary agencies, trade unions, etc.) and especially to the State(s)? What is the special role of the Christian laity?

(c) How can persons, communities, and social structures be changed? From theological tradition and pastoral experience the Church can contribute insights into the modes of conversion of individuals and groups. For instance, through its missionary work it also has some experience as an agent of change in society. Underlying questions remain: How does reorientation to God and one's neighbour relate? What is the interaction between personal change and that of social structures and institutions?

C. SOURCES FOR THEOLOGICAL STUDY

The theological issues posed by development point to source materials in the Bible and theological tradition to which further study has to give attention. The sources are of two types:

1. Major theological themes.
2. Particular theological topics.

1. *Major theological themes*

(a) *Christology*

Here lies the key to a great number of theological issues raised – in Christology we find the clearest indication of what the new man and renewed humanity is to be (see Uppsala Report, Section II).

With this double perspective in mind particular sources in Christology are of special significance:

(i) The Adam-Christ parallel and all sources referring to the 'new creation' in Christ, to his 'sonship' as well as the Gospel narrative of how he in fact expressed in attitude, teaching, and action the being of the 'new man'.

(ii) The tension between the universality of Christ's ministry and the particularity of incarnation accepting certain historical cultural, and social conditions and limitations, yet transforming them into ultimate humanity.

(iii) Christ's relationship to his neighbours, his service in society as recorded in the Gospels and reflected in the theological and ethical statements of the Epistles.

(iv) The interaction between the three ministries of Christ, as King, Priest, and Prophet. (Are there other elements in his ministry which traditional theological teaching has not sufficiently emphasized?)

(b) *Anthropology*

One element already present in Christology needs to be further drawn out: the Hebrew-Christian understanding of man and of his identity. The following strands are of importance:

(i) The *imago dei* quality given to man in creation and restored by Christ. This means exploration of the three aspects of *imago*: the 'sonship' of man as compared with Christ's; partnership with God in dominion over the earth; and man as an integral part of the whole cosmos. On all these aspects Patristic theology has much to say as we listen to man's search for identity today.

(ii) Man seen in terms of his activity, all materials dealing with responsible and just action beginning with the creation mandate, continuing through the prophetic message to New Testament teachings, admonitions, and exhortations. What is the continuity in the revelation of moral directives for man?

(iii) Man seen in terms of suffering. The rich sources of biblical material on the role of suffering and in particular on vicarious suffering of the people of God, of the suffering servant, and the meaning for man and society of suffering focused in the Cross, all have an immediate bearing on the dignity of man, the inter-dependence of privileged and poor, the spiritual contribution of cross-bearing to human development.

(iv) Man seen in terms of his relationships: personal, communal, and civic, but also local and universal. Much of the same material mentioned above will deepen understanding of man's social nature according to Christian anthropology. However, beyond the tradi-tional approach, special attention should focus on man's 'relation-ship' to social and organizational structures, especially the possibility of 'alienation' and 'dehumanization' by 'destructive structures' – biblically speaking the question of 'powers and principalities' as an aspect of transpersonal evil.

(v) Man seen in terms of the quality of his community and personal life. The question of what is the salvation offered to man must be pursued here. Can we give a coherent description of the 'liberation to and from' which is offered in Christ? The Pauline theological teaching on justification by faith as well as the Johannine message of a 'liberated life in Christ' need to be evaluated again in this context.

(c) *Ecclesiology*

'Christology' and 'anthropology' have already pointed to many strands of 'ecclesiology'. The three form one interlocking theme. However, with 'ecclesiology' we enter controversial ground ecumenically and it will be very difficult to reach a principle consensus.

Yet accepting a number of different types of 'ecclesiology' it should be possible to pursue the following tasks together:

(i) To clarify the mode of the Church's presence in the world. A large part of that clarification depends on a better understanding of the biblical term 'world', in its three dimensions: world as nature, world as history, and world as society. Many studies have already been undertaken. The main task of evaluating them systematically remains to be done.

(ii) The tension and dynamic interaction between the Church's diverse ministries – priestly, prophetic, etc. – in relation to Christ's three ministries should be further studied. A great deal seems to depend on whether the Church will manage to keep its various tasks in a creative tension to each other rather than to opt only for one of them or to neutralize each by avoiding tensions.

(iii) The notion of the Church as *pars pro toto* could be further explored. Exegetically the focus is on the understanding of 'elec-tion' in the Old and New Testaments and on the Church's calling to be the beginning of a new mankind, e.g. the calling of the twelve disciples to be representatives of the new Israel, the references to 'first-fruit', 'chosen race', etc. Systematically, one needs to bring into connection the Church as a community without geographical, cultural, and social boundaries ('neither Jew nor Greek') and the nature of its fellowship being built on diverse gifts, containing social, cultural, and geographical elements.

(d) *Eschatology*

Moltmann's paper will lift up this particular theme. Here we need only a few remarks:

(i) It would be helpful to work on a typology of different eschatologies.

(ii) It will be important to establish clear guidelines within which any interpretation must fall, e.g. it cannot ignore incarnation and the historicity of God's action, it must not pervert eschatology into an immanent historic process which will bring about the Kingdom in this time and world, etc.

(iii) The nature of the 'new' in comparison to the 'old', the historic shape of renewal initiated by the resurrection of Christ, needs to be spelled out.

(iv) What are the realizable signs of the future towards which all 'development' must move? How should the short-, middle-, and long-range goals of development relate to those signs?

2. *Particular theological topics*

In relation to the major themes some particular topics require special study. In each case the source material will be found in a cross-section of biblical literature.

(a) A biblical and theological phenomenology of the understanding of 'nations'.

(b) An evaluation of the role and calling of the laity, i.e. non-institutional forms of Christian participation in development.

(c) Study of the biblical notion of 'principalities and powers' in relation to institutional and organizational structures in modern society.

(d) Study of the problem of violence in relation to a situation in which 'just wars/revolutions' are no longer possible, but which, however, is on the other hand characterized by conflicts of interest between different groups and nations which inevitably lead to violent confrontations.

(e) A re-study of the relation between 'law', 'order', and 'justice' in a pluralistic society (most traditional teaching assumes a homogeneous, paternalistic society of a pre-French Revolution type).

(f) Study of the meaning of 'reconciliation' in a world society based on inevitable and necessary (to generate the impetus for development) tensions in which the Church cannot remain neutral or harmonize but must take sides, yet must transcend individual interests and have the whole in mind.

(g) A radically new appraisal of the prophetic calling in the Christian church. What makes a prophet? What are his corresponding roles in society and in the Church? Who are the bearers of the calling – individuals, teams, movements – and what is their relation to the establishment of the institutional Church? How can the prophetic challenge reach transpersonal power structures?

D. METHODOLOGY

The approach taken in this paper makes certain methodological assumptions:

1. In order to isolate the theological issues posed by development we cannot follow either a merely deductive method, i.e. start from given positions in the biblical theology and teaching tradition of the Church, or follow a purely inductive method, i.e. take social, economic, and political analysis as the only point of departure for theological reflection. The assumption is rather that we must establish a 'dialectical interaction' between the issues of development as they are posed in the secular discussion and theological thinking.

2. In looking for theological source materials, I tried to beware of overemphasis of particular isolated strands of biblical teaching which would give strong, yet narrow support to certain aspects of development. Instead, I have attempted to identify the major theological themes which have a bearing on the issues posed by development and to interpret them as much as possible in the total context of the Christian faith.

3. In dealing with biblical materials, the hermeneutical question is inevitably raised. Some ground work has already been done on it in relation to social ethics. However, a good deal more needs to be done and a special working group may be required, bringing together Old Testament and New Testament exegetes with representatives of social ethics and social sciences.

4. It is clearly not satisfactory to identify theological issues and source materials without more discussion on the type of theological statements which are possible and desirable as a result of further studies. Underlying the theological discussion there are different presuppositions of what the Christian Church should and could say

and do. They must be brought into the open:

(a) The traditional way of making theological statements and ecclesial pronouncements is challenged on the grounds of their all-comprehensive irrelevance and lack of sensitivity to the complex technical and scientific issues involved. What are the continuing possibilities and limitations of such theological statements, consensus reports, etc.?

(b) The social ethics discussion is characterized by sharp contrasts and disagreements within and between Christian churches. Every ecumenical discussion has therefore to deal with the methodological questions: how can minority opinions be made heard without relativizing the majority position? How do we proceed in cases of substantial disagreement? Methodological proposals like the use of a typology, i.e. the comparative listing of different approaches and solutions, have been made. Their usefulness for the work of the consultation should be examined.

Nikos A. Nissiotis · *Introduction to a Christological Phenomenology of Development*

Nikos A. Nissiotis, 'Introduction to a Christological Phenomenology of Development', *Technology and Social Justice* ed. Ronald H. Preston, SCM Press, London and Judson Press, Valley Forge 1971, pp.148-55

The word theology is very often used in the sense of a theological approach to a concrete phenomenon in the world concerning human relationship. In this sense one can definitely say that there is a theological phenomenology, inasmuch as one tries to find in God the deeper sense of a phenomenon in the light of one's faith in him and his relationship to historical events. I do not mean ethical or sociological thinking which elaborates principles of human behaviour on the basis of the Bible and Christian experience in contemporary society; this preoccupation could be named theology *for* development, and would have as its purpose the preparing of churches and individuals for action in view of today's developments. This theology for development is self-evident and essential for all churches today. In this paper, however, I am dealing with something that to my mind precedes this stage. It is the theological sense of development, namely that of looking at development through faith in Christ and his incarnation. A theological phenomenology of this kind seems to me to be absolutely necessary as the prelude to all social involvement on the part of the churches, and their responsible action as churches in the contemporary explosion of science and technology. To a great extent the church's role within today's continuing social change will depend on how we as Christians understand development in relationship to God's continuous creativity towards the completion of his creation. Only then can one speak of a theology of development in this strict phenomenological sense and in close relationship to what is basic theology.

Theology is not just phenomenology or communication. Etymologically it refers to a word about God, that is to say, systematic thinking about God and his revelation. In the narrow sense of the term one is obliged as a theologian to limit oneself within the boundaries that God prescribes; that is, after the incarnation of the Word of God, our word cannot remain an abstract philosophical reflection about God. It refers to the Word incarnate in history; and therefore the task of theology is to be a reflection on God's presence in history. Theology, then, is the thinking of God as he reveals himself to man and the world; it deals with God's being in time and in concrete personal action.

Systematic theology, then, signifies the systematization of the biblical revelation. No one can deny this fundamental approach of theology, but no one can pretend today that the task of theology – understood as the apprehension of the fullness of the reality of the incarnate Logos of God – can remain only within these limits. Not only Christian ethics or the philosophy of religion as extensions of dogmatics are necessary, but the whole concrete cosmos, its culture and civilization, its progress and evolution, the human condition and concrete historical events are inseparable elements in a theology of incarnation.

I want to insist, however, that all these are not additional or separate chapters of theology in a post-biblical era. Theological phenomenology, as a critical study of the historical phenomena in the light of the incarnation, is rooted in and inseparably linked with the substance of the historical personal revelation of God. This is important for two reasons: first, that no distance or opposition is introduced between the so-called vertical and horizontal lines, between the Word of God incarnate and the reality of this world; and secondly, that no substitute for the revelation itself and the biblical message of salvation is professed, as might be implied in the view which says that in a post-biblical era the agenda of theology is written by the world alone. Here we touch the crucial issue of today's ecumenical debate and we have to clarify it before we attempt any kind of theological phenomenology of development ...

The current historical situation is a first point of contact for a theological phenomenology. But if we remain only at this point of departure, without seeking to see its special meaning in the light of the revealed personal God as a source of grace and judgment, then we can no longer speak of a theology of development, but only of a new type of humanism and natural theology. What distinguishes an authentic theology of development from such a humanism or a natural theology is not an abstract escape to a theistic God or to metaphysics or even to a static concept of salvation understood as expiation from our sins; but it is the ability to discern the signs of the times according to the edifying and saving judgment of God, acting in Christ and present in the Spirit through the church in all realms of the personal and collective life of man. In other words, the attitude of the horizontalists should not be corrected by a static theology of the Word or a separate, remote and wholly transcendental (and therefore unattainable) reality. It should be corrected by seeing things in themselves and in their relationships as basic materials of complex historical events which are brought under the judgment of God. We then have a theology *of* development accessible through a theological phenomenology; namely through investigating the logos (the cause and the reason) of being and the purpose of phenomena, not only by one's own conscience, experience, and intellectual possibilities of grasping the ultimate realities of a transcendental order, but in God's judgment and grace. In this way no opposition between verticalists and horizontalists, between transcendentalists and immanentists is possible, because in historical reality a Christian traces the dynamics of God and proceeds to an evaluation of it in the light of Christ's presence.

Whoever grasps the distinctive act of God in Christ cannot but trace it as an ongoing historical reality. The horizontal line for the Christian faith contains the vertical, and *vice versa*. The one does not send us for completion to the other, but they coexist as an inseparable whole. The distinction between the two is made because they belong together in Christ's event; it is also made in order to reaffirm the unity between the two in an authentic Christian approach to a concrete historical event, so that in each case we might operate with a realistic theological discernment, preparing the churches for appropriate involvement and action.

The question raised is, therefore, not What is development? but

What is its cause, its *raison d'être* and its goal in God's judgment? If we call to mind the various definitions of development in general as 'the autonomous activity of man to achieve a higher standard of dignity and material sufficiency', or 'the totality of processes by which individual human beings and human societies seek constantly to realize their potentialities', then we are given a positive starting-point for grasping the theological meaning of this phenomenon in God. But we have immediately to make the following observations:

(a) Development is both material and spiritual.

(b) It is individual and collective.

(c) It is quantitative and qualitative.

In other words development concerns the whole man and his whole environment, and consequently one rightly speaks of a total effort of humanization. In Christ this effort finds its deepest *raison d'être* and purpose. It would be wrong to think of this effort as merely autonomous – though it is autonomous as a purely human operation – either in its functional reality or in its means for achieving the goal. A theological phenomenology of development does not question whether there is an autonomy of operation, but seeks the deeper sense of development in God as the Lord of history. Development is a God-given possibility to man for making him a collaborator towards the completion of God's creation, through man's link with God in Christ. This struggle of humanity towards its full dignity reveals that man and the world are created with a specific purpose, with a goal to be attained through a continuous process of change and renewal. That goal is the reality which has been revealed by God in this world in the person of Jesus ...

On the basis of these preliminary remarks we can see that from the Christian point of view every aspect of development and every aspect of human progress cannot be exhausted by the mere registering that it is in fact taking place. We have to penetrate beneath the surface, beneath its simple functioning, and try to find its deeper significance for total human existence in a responsible society. It is in this phenomenological operation that the theology of development is operating for the sake of development itself. In each event, phase and aspect of it God's will is revealed in a special way for all men; it becomes manifest how God's will is incarnate and how Christ's regenerating power can be appropriated as the inner power of the world's history. God is no longer an abstract ethical principle guiding action from a distance. He is the heart of the event, the human person involved in a dynamic action for the progress of all creation. In this sense we should not speak of

a theological phenomenology of development but of a christological one.

This inner power of development constitutes the backbone of
history in the movement forward to its completion. It is the inner
sense of life, the being of man turned towards the achievement of
a higher degree of human personality. Christ, the inner sense of
development, and the human being, all three are related through
the concrete historical events. These events reveal the origin, meaning and purpose of the whole creation. Therefore one has to trace
the reality and the meaning of all these phases of development
and thus reveal their inner coherence. These are some of the
significant aspects of a developmental event:

(*a*) It has international and universal dimensions and never
merely national or individual ones.

(*b*) It abolishes discrimination between the privileged and the
under-privileged.

(*c*) It poses the problem of defeating injustice in the distribution
of the earth's goods and the fruits of technical civilization.

(*d*) It contributes to the maintenance of peace, by overcoming
the fighting between oppressors and oppressed and the dependence
of developing upon developed nations.

(*e*) It sets up new possibilities for world-wide education and
the growth of human personality.

(*f*) It reveals the fact that all events involving human progress
are not ends in themselves, concerning only material welfare, but
that they are above all means for creating human personality and
moving history forward for the sake of future generations.

It becomes more and more clear that the accumulation of progress and development through technological change in itself leaves
many other problems unsolved. These are becoming more complicated the more development increases. A christological
phenomenology has to detect the reasons why this is so by remind-
ing us that development means more than progress seen as the
result of economic relationships.

Let us now investigate how a christological phenomenology of
development detects the reasons for the problems caused by development. Usually Christian theologians in modern times operate a
theology of development by extending the meaning of the incarnation in the secular realm. The incarnation is then understood as an
event which refers not only to the church, as the renewed people of
God which resulted from it, but also to the whole world and its
history. This interpretation is not absolutely wrong, although from

a theological point of view the incarnation cannot be used alone in order to approach the riddle of history. In other words, one cannot provide the necessary basis for a theology of development without the cross and the resurrection, as well as the foundation of the historical community of faith. A full reference is needed to all stages of the divine economy as seen christologically. The christological phenomenology of development, of which the premisses are described above, cannot operate unless an appropriate understanding of salvation in Christ is used as the basic reality when we reflect on human progress in history. Salvation proves here to be the depth dimension of development which is the missing element in its simple function and completion ...

Two remarks are to be made here. First, sacred and profane are not two opposed or separated realms. The sacred is the secular understood at a deep level. Secondly, the vision of salvation extended into the secular is based on the particular intervention of God in Christ, whose salvation reveals that every historical event contains a possibility of becoming an agent of this salvation if it acquires the broad dimension given to it by Christ's incarnation, death and resurrection. A historical event acquires its deeper significance in the eyes of a Christian only when it really assists in the restoration of humanity to all men according to the cosmic understanding of the reality of Christ's salvation. This is not automatically given to every historical event. A service to humanity as a whole is a highly complicated affair which cannot be reduced only to the limits of a welfare programme of economic and social change. There is always something missing in the eyes of a Christian phenomenologist. This can be captured only if the event is transformed into a service to man, i.e. if the event extends the salvation of Christ understood as a vehicle for the regeneration of history.

Cosmic salvation in this sense does not mean a mystical and speculative vision conceiving the whole creation as automatically saved because Christ died for all men. This is a vague generalization. In reality it does not do justice to specific historical events and the human responsibility in them. It eliminates the judging elements which is at the heart of Christ's salvation. 'Cosmic' in my view points to a worldly and world-wide salvation through a strenuous, continuous process of inner transformation, conceivable only in the faith, love and hope given in Christ in a personal, concrete way. The cosmic vision is not possible without the cosmic reality of salvation as regeneration, as continuous change in order that every historical event comes under the saving judgment of Jesus. If it is to further development each historical event has to be seen in its appropriate function in order to serve man's personal transfiguration and society's total restructuring.

All events connected with development await their evaluation and, through it, their appropriate function in this cosmic understanding of salvation, which unites the personal and the social, the cosmic and the secular, the sacred and the profane. According to a Christian phenomenology of development Christ provides, through the faith of the man who acts in faith, the missing basis of development and enables it to make a more positive contribution to regenerating the world.

There is in other words a cosmic Christian vision of the secular and the universal but this has very little to do with a theoretical, speculative and visionary interpretation of the salvation of all things in Christ. In reality the appropriate practice deriving from the universal salvation of Christ is a specific Christian contribution in all these historical events. Human activism and technological change do not solve the problems of justice, peace and universal partnership in development. There is no automatic presence of Christ in development. The more we develop human resources, the more we need specific Christian participation. The only generalized principle which can be applied is that Christians should approach the phenomenology of development with a positive mind and a concern for all that furthers material and economic growth at the service of man. They know that the judgment of God in history, through the regenerating spirit of Christ, is never annihilating, but constructive and saving. In Christ we and every event are judged. In him we know that justice and love are absolutely interchangeable, even though we cannot fully understand how this is so. Our concept of justice includes punishment as an inseparable part. We cannot conceive a loving justice in an absolute form as is the case with God; we cannot see how the world's history can be saved in love and judgment by God ...

The true regenerating contribution of the Christian to development has to be a balance between the extremes of easy optimistic cosmic visions of a 'secular' Christianity and of the welfare policies of affluent societies, and the pessimistic theologies of the sin of man, of his condemnation, of the vanity of history and the tragedy of the human condition.

Paulo Tufari · *The Church between Ideology and Utopia*

Paulo Tufari, SJ, 'The Church between Ideology and Utopia', *Theology Meets Progress* ed. Philip Land, Gregorian University Press, Rome 1971, pp.256-65

The Will to Transform Reality

Is theology of development truly utopian, or is it 'ideological', that is serving 'the purpose of glossing over or stabilizing the existing social reality?' Those writing theologically about human progress declare their intention of setting in motion processes of innovation that may go so far as to embrace the so-called revolutionary hypothesis.

But verbal declarations, as everyone knows, sometimes conceal (and scarcely ever reveal) one's full intention. Hence arises the need of considering *implicit assumptions* lying beyond the formal declarations. Implicit assumptions may be defined as feelings, needs, convictions and aspirations which, while not entering formally into programmatic declarations, actually influence both their theoretical formulation and the procedures for accomplishing them.

What is at issue is not the disclosure of unconscious motives or secret reasons of particular persons. For our approach is neither ethical nor psychoanalytical. In what follows, we draw attention to certain *general conditions of life which presumably affect the type of people who appear to be most active in promoting theology of development.*

Take first the social status of these. Is it reasonable to expect that there will be an effective will 'to transform the existing order of life' on the part of people who have as a rule achieved their professional competence within a well-established cultural tradition who speak in the name of an officially recognized institution – the Church; and who may hold prestigious posts in organizations requiring financial support for their activities whether national or international? Can this transforming be hoped for from people whose profession and programmes are, if not dependent on, certainly facilitated by the continued functioning of the very structures which must, according to their verbal declarations, be transformed if a new and more equitable social order is to be realized?

Our question should not surprise. It is only an application of that more general sociological problem of whether a substantial process of change can ever be initiated within a system, by its very representatives, where 'system' signifies allocation of economic resources, hierarchy of power and theoretical legitimation of both.

Next we raise a question that emerges from the historical circumstances in which theology of development has taken shape. The 'verbal declaration' would have it that this theological movement stems from the Church's awareness that she can and must take a stand in support of the masses striving to attain the benefits which thus far only the few have gained through cultural, social and welfare organization. The fact of critical disparity of income between poor lands and rich lands is everywhere recognized. The Church's concern over this disparity can surely not be denied. At the same time, it is also a fact that the Church finds herself growingly estranged from the world of cultural and social organization which seeks to humanize life. For this reason surveys are multiplied to search out a more meaningful role for priests in a secularized society, while other artistic and anthropological enquiries seek to make old rites more meaningful for modern man.

Theology of development has grown up in association with these factors. Is the association merely casual, or is it also to some extent causal? Some will inevitably be inclined to presume that (at the level of implicit assumptions) the theological endeavour is intended not only to help men overcome alienation from the benefits of culture but also to help the Church surmount her own cultural alienation from men. Support for this hypothesis is found in the introduction into the vocabulary of this theology of words and expressions already made fashionable in certain philosophical circles and political movements. Consider, for instance, the search for appealing titles and new designations, with the result that to an already inflated list of 'theologies' that include those of 'leisure' and of 'urban behaviour,' of 'technocratic structures' and 'human transplants,' of 'tourism' and of 'sex,' we now add 'theology' of liberation, of revolution, of violence. These are just a few examples drawn from a picturesque list of titles published by catholic theological reviews in the last two years. One could take exception to the very idea of theologizing about the most disparate aspects of human existence. But apart from this normative question, the point here is that the very choice of words and topics seems to make plausible the hypothesis that theology of development seeks to make itself interesting to a society which in different ways shows no interest in Churchly pronouncements. Surely, the hint is slight, but the hypothesis is worthy of being tested, since it is intimately connected with the basic query as to whether theology of development really intends to transform the existing order or is rather an ideology meant 'to serve the purpose of glossing over or stabilizing the existing social reality.' Should such a hypothesis be confirmed, then theology of development could be rightly considered a particular instance of that process by which *well established institutions tend to transform the symbols of their presence according to changing circumstances in order to preserve unchanged their acquired ascendancy.*

An analysis of these two conditions – social status and historical context – might on rigorous inquiry reveal a certain inconsistency between verbal declarations and implicit assumptions in the case of theology of development. *A priori*, this cannot be excluded. What, however, can be excluded *a priori*, and must, is the assumption that such inconsistency is always a sign of illicit motivation or of vested interests. For it remains altogether possible that people, while influenced by their existential conditions, choose nevertheless to work for values of their faith rather than for their private interests. To deny this possibility is to fall into a social determinism as dogmatic as it is pseudo-scientific.

Let it be recognized, then, that among promoters of theology of development it is possible to find a basic ideological orientation (at the level of implicit assumptions) together with typically utopian traits (insofar as regards consciously-pursued goals). How people manage to operate effectively when they are caught in such inconsistency between immediate self-interests and fundamental religious values is another matter. Still, perhaps we can count as one utopian trait of theology of development this conscious determination to pursue goals and ideals under conditions that many consider either impossible or unacceptable.

The Capacity to Transform Reality

For theology to qualify as utopian, besides the proclamation of its message, it must possess the objective capacity to 'transform *de facto* the existing reality into one more in accord with its own conceptions.'

The principle is clear, but in fact raises difficult problems concerning the analysis of social causality. In our case the question appears even more intricate, because the phenomenon under consideration affects people in widely different cultural contexts, let alone the fact that the whole process is still developing. We must, accordingly, limit ourselves to altogether tentative considerations about implications of present efforts to 'orient conduct towards elements which the situation, insofar as it is realized at the time, does not contain.'

In the first place, the power of a utopia lies less in the intrinsic reason the message contains than in the feeling of commitment that the message is capable of arousing. To transform reality the utopian message must 'orient conduct' in a way that evokes both ethos and pathos so as to provoke action on the part of the many to the benefit of all.

Has theology of development such power of evocation and provocation? One is prone to doubt it, considering the abstractness of certain theological papers; consider in addition those carefully balanced official pronouncements which speak about the urgent need for courageous action without conveying either a sense of urgency or courage to act. In view of these considerations, the doubt appears reasonable, but surely more empirical study is needed before we transform our plausible hypothesis into a definite assertion.

At any rate this is not the only nor is it the most relevant way of considering the question. In fact, one must always bear in mind that no judgment is valid that considers only results without weighing costs. The heart of the matter, therefore, concerns not so much the capacity of achieving certain effects as the hazards involved in such an achievement.

Let us consider one case in particular, namely, the risk that theology of development may arrive at stressing its own thesis at the cost of other Christian values and alternative orientations. The risk does not seem merely hypothetical. In point of fact, one cannot escape the impression that writings on theology of development tend to ignore or at least to play down a number of relevant aspects which do not fit into the simplified scheme of a Church deeply concerned with social progress in the present world. A scheme like this makes difficult the insertion of certain aspects which are typical and proper to the Christian calling. By way of illustration, let us mention: renunciation of visible goods in favour of hope in the world to come; the call to a contemplative style of life alien to any utilitarian view of time, nature and knowledge; the supreme importance of the individual as individual, attainable only through the personal bonds of long-lived friendship. In a world, all that is ultimate rather than instrumental, understandable but not explainable, supremely important and yet not directly useful; in St. Thomas' terms, the act of *frui* over and above the actions of *uti*.

This list is neither systematic nor exhaustive. It was drawn up on the basis of preliminary observations which a more accurate analysis might confirm, modify or even prove basically incorrect. But there is one thing which needs neither confirmation nor proof. This is that the values just listed are so essential to the Christian calling that their loss would undermine the very foundation of the Church's self-identity.

Of course, the same can be said of doctrines which simplify the Christian message in the opposite direction – the so-called vertical dimension. However, at the present moment the latter is a more remote possibility, given the unpopularity of any teaching which does not extol 'terrestrial realities.'

Our line of enquiry may lead one to conclude that theology of development suffers from a built-in contradiction. On the one hand, to be effective, it has to present a simplified message in terms of social needs and needed social action. On the other, this very simplification entails the risk of rendering meaningless the ultimate foundation on which the 'theology' rests. Should such a price be paid, no one would claim that theology of development – however appealing and influential – was succeeding 'in transforming reality into one more in accord with *its own* conceptions.'

The contradiction exists and must be solved in concrete situations which demand choice and action. For at a purely theoretical level there is no particular difficulty in recognizing that Christianity cannot be reduced to any unilateral understanding of the individual and his society, of time and eternity, reason and mystery. And always a theoretical analysis can expound these polarities simultaneously showing their complementarity. The real difficulty arises when judgment must be made in concrete situations as to which of these polarities should receive preference and where appropriate action should be taken in order to direct the course of events towards the preferred direction.

Therefore theology of development – like any other doctrine meant to orient conduct and determine action – has to take sides in favour of what at the present appears more urgent. This implies unbalancing the theoretical equilibrium of the complementary polarities proper to the Christian message so as to arrive at an operative interpretation of specific, impelling human problems. But this should never be at the cost of elevating such warranted interpretations into universally valid absolutes, lest the totality of the

Christian mystery as well as the pluralism of personal callings should be misconceived.

The capacity to be selective without becoming unilateral is a crucial test of any form of knowledge which aims at giving a significant representation of a complex situation. The test is all the more severe in the case of those movements of thought which – for being utopian – aim 'to inspire collective activity' in order 'to change such reality to conform with their goals which transcend reality.'

Should the theology of development manifest *de facto* such capacity, it could properly be judged utopian; and this not on the basis of any *a priori* value-judgment nor in view of any sociological definition, but on the basis of the historical evidence which shows that seldom or ever has 'the existing order of reality' been transformed by a doctrine that was radical but not demagogic, mindful of social necessity without being utilitarian, centred on the absolute respect for the individual, and yet not aristocratic.

5· Theology of Liberation

The development debate was concentrated on the period 1968-71 and still continues. The issue of development is arguably the most important one to face mankind since the days of Noah, yet as we have seen there is pessimism in the underdeveloped world at the prospects for development. There is also cynicism about the fine words contributed to the debate by nations responsible for maintaining the present inequities. The idea and possibility of development excite less today and the very term 'development' has in some areas a distinctly hollow ring. Especially in Latin America 'developmentism' is a derogatory term.

'Revolution' focused attention on the necessity for qualitative change at the most fundamental levels, levels of values, aspirations and self-understanding. It underlined the necessity of dealing with the structural impediments to a new future. It exposed the institutionalized opposition to an alternative way for man. But the term revolution had at least for Western ears connotations which were unacceptable and frightening. For this reason the idea of development was taken up with enthusiasm. Indeed the Third World must have been suspicious of the term for this reason alone. It was the very acceptability of the idea of development that proved its limitations. It suited the white north rather well. The idea of development was indeed enthusiastically proposed instead of revolution. It had about it the assurance of rationality, continuity with the patterns of the past, control and measurable goals. Development was essentially about quantitative change along the well-trodden path of the north. It was less emotive and 'political' than revolution. Above all it promised that no matter what change took place the north would always be superior and the south always dependent. 'Development is the new name for peace', declared Cardinal Feltin. But given bad faith in the north, development became the guarantee that the new day would never dawn.

Those who have most to lose find the preservation of the present strangely peaceful.

In Latin America and indeed throughout the underdeveloped world the term 'liberation' has displaced the idea of development. There is more than semantic significance in this change. The lessons of revolution and development have not been forgotten. Neither term was subtle enough to gather up all the dimensions now associated with liberation. The change in terminology itself is indicative of that process of conscientization associated with Latin America. Through long experience, much of it bitter experience, the level of consciousness has been raised about the true goals on which attention should be focused and the real obstacles to their attainment.

Liberation preserves the dimension of qualitative change associated with revolution. But if it includes the concrete, the large and objective forces of oppression in its analysis, it also points to the area of the personal and even spiritual dimensions. It gathers up the humanization stage of the development debate. It is not concerned with impressive edifices built on unexamined foundations. But it guards more carefully than the term revolution, against superficial change which affects only the external conditions of life.

One of the most important aspects of conscientization – practical raising of consciousness in the light of experience and reflection – is the realization that life in the Third World, especially in Latin America, is to be characterized by the term 'dependence'. Clearly there is economic dependence, and we have already noted this in discussing development. The poor countries are dependent on the rich for aid, for trade and for technology. Liberation from economic dependence is necessary before any development can take place. Here liberation includes the element of revolution because no one should be under any illusions about the forces which will try to prevent the breaking of dependence. If the developed world is to continue to enjoy its standard of living then economic independence must not be allowed. It is for this reason that in Latin America there are grounds for seeing American political and economic interests working hand in hand.

But there is also a form of cultural dependence in a wide sense. The concept of liberation also means liberation from the automatic acceptance of the ideas and values of the developed world: the dominant ideas of the dominant powers. Obviously the acceptance of these ideas tends to a perpetuation of economic dependence, for it is only through following the model of economic development that the poor countries can achieve the affluence of the rich countries. But as we have seen the model and the goals of the rich countries are now being questioned elsewhere. Liberation means the possibility of developing alternative societies which aim at quite different goals from affluence and Western materialism.

The theology of liberation must be viewed within this context of cultural dependence. Western theology has dominated the thinking and the practice of the churches throughout the world. It is very interesting to see now a criticism of that theology from within the Christian experience of the Third World. Although the Roman Catholic Church has been very influential in Latin America (and the conjunction of Roman and Latin here is not to be underestimated) the influence has until recently been, if anything, on the side of dependence rather than liberation. But in the late 1960s at least some of the bishops began to make statements on social and economic matters, as they affected the lives of the people. For example there is the famous 'Letter to the Peoples of the Third World', signed by eighteen bishops from all over the Third World, issued in 1967. Most of the new thinking among Latin American bishops has been in connection with CELAM (the General Conference of Latin American Bishops) especially the conference at Medellin, Colombia, in 1968.

There is a third, and more subtle area of dependence, namely the dependence experienced *within* nations. The south's relations with the north are repeated this time in the dependence of each country on the capital. Ironically, the south is not dependent on the north fundamentally, but rather artificially. The rich countries are actually dependent on the poor countries for their continued prosperity. The capital is actually dependent on the regions for its prosperity, but there is a myth about that the regions are indebted to the capital. Through conscientization this myth is exposed, and dependence is attacked. Liberation therefore begins at home. The 'marginals' live what are described as less-than-human lives. The country is not run in such a way that they can be integrated with any progress that is made. Naturally there is a community of interest between many of those in the capital and the powerful forces of the rich world. Those in the capital may well share the values and ideas of the rich world. Liberation, which incorporates the concern for development, must face the question about those who, out of self-interest, prevent the liberation of the nation. What happens when the minority will not allow the vast majority to progress towards their own future?

Once again we must recall that although Fanon was an advocate of violence in such a situation, he was also conscious of the need for reconciliation. He had a special interest in the liberation of the West from its own dehumanizing ways. He said it was the task of the Third World to liberate the West. Today in Latin America there is a real attempt to face the question of what to do with and how to relate to those who happily perpetuate the life of the marginals as less-than-humans. How is the oppressor to be liberated from his own inhumanity? The movement for liberation points us back to a deeper understanding of the cross and resurrection.

Gustavo Gutierrez · *A Spirituality of Liberation*

Gustavo Gutierrez, *A Theology of Liberation*, SCM Press, London 1974 and Orbis Books, Maryknoll 1973, pp.203-208

To place oneself in the perspective of the Kingdom means to participate in the struggle for the liberation of those oppressed by others. This is what many Christians who have committed themselves to the Latin American revolutionary process have begun to experience. If this option seems to separate them from the Christian community, it is because many Christians, intent on domesticating the Good News, see them as wayward and perhaps even dangerous. If they are not always able to express in appropriate terms the profound reasons for their commitment, it is because the theology in which they were formed – and which they share with other Christians – has not produced the categories necessary to express this option, which seeks to respond creatively to the new demands of the Gospel and of the oppressed and exploited peoples of this continent. But in their commitments, and even in their attempts to explain them, there is a greater understanding of the faith, greater faith, greater fidelity to the Lord than in the 'orthodox' doctrine (some prefer to call it by this name) of reputable Christian circles. This doctrine is supported by authority and much publicized because of access to social communications media, but it is so static and devitalized that it is not even strong enough to abandon the Gospel. It is the Gospel which is disowning it.

But theological categories are not enough. We need a vital attitude, all-embracing and synthesizing, informing the totality as well as every detail of our lives; we need a 'spirituality.' Spirituality, in the strict and profound sense of the word is the dominion of the Spirit. If 'the truth will set you free' (John 8:32), the Spirit 'will guide you into all the truth' (John 16:13) and will lead us to complete freedom, the freedom from everything that hinders us from fulfilling ourselves as men and sons of God and the freedom to love and to enter into communion with God and with others. It will lead us along the path of liberation because 'where the Spirit of the Lord is, there is liberty' (2 Cor. 3:17).

A spirituality is a concrete manner, inspired by the Spirit, of living the Gospel; it is a definite way of living 'before the Lord,' in solidarity with all men, 'with the Lord,' and before men. It arises from an intense spiritual experience, which is later explicated and witnessed to. Some Christians are beginning to live this experience as a result of their commitment to the process of liberation. The experiences of previous generations are there to support it, but above all, to remind them that they must discover their own way. Not only is there a contemporary history and a contemporary Gospel; there is also a contemporary spiritual experience which cannot be overlooked. A spirituality means a reordering of the great axes of the Christian life in terms of this contemporary experience. What is new is the synthesis that this reordering brings about, in stimulating a deepened understanding of various ideas, in bringing to the surface unknown or forgotten aspects of the Christian life, and above all, in the way in which these things are converted into life, prayer, commitment, and action.

The truth is that a Christianity lived in commitment to the process of liberation presents its own problems which cannot be ignored and meets obstacles which must be overcome. For many, the encounter with the Lord under these conditions can disappear by giving way to what he himself brings forth and nourishes: love for man. This love, however, does not know the fullness of its potential. This is a real difficulty, but the solution must come from the heart of the problem itself. Otherwise, it would be just one more patchwork remedy, a new impasse. This is the challenge confronting a spirituality of liberation. Where oppression and the liberation of man seem to make God irrelevant – a God filtered by our longtime indifference to these problems – there must blossom faith and hope in him who comes to root out injustice and to offer, in an unforeseen way, total liberation. This is a spirituality which dares to sink roots in the soil of oppression-liberation.

A spirituality of liberation will centre on a *conversion* to the neighbour, the oppressed person, the exploited social class, the despised race, the dominated country. Our conversion to the Lord implies this conversion to the neighbour. Evangelical conversion is indeed the touchstone of all spirituality. Conversion means a radical transformation of ourselves; it means thinking, feeling, and living as Christ – present in exploited and alienated man. To be converted is to commit oneself to the process of the liberation of the poor and oppressed, to commit oneself lucidly, realistically, and concretely. It means to commit oneself not only generously. but also with an analysis of the situation and a strategy of action. To be converted is to know and experience the fact that, contrary to the laws of physics, we can stand straight, according to the Gospel, only when our centre of gravity is outside ourselves.

Conversion is a permanent process in which very often the obstacles we meet make us lose all we had gained and start anew. The fruitfulness of our conversion depends on our openness to doing this, our spiritual childhood. All conversion implies a break. To wish to accomplish it without conflict is to deceive oneself and others: 'No man is worthy of me who cares more for father or mother than for me.' But it is not a question of a withdrawn and pious attitude. Our conversion process is affected by the socio-economic, political, cultural, and human environment in which it occurs. Without a change in these structures, there is no authentic conversion. We have to break with our mental categories, with the way we relate to others, with our way of identifying with the Lord, with our cultural milieu, with our social class, in other words, with all that can stand in the way of a real, profound solidarity with those who suffer, in the first place, from misery and injustice. Only thus, and not through purely interior and spiritual attitudes, will the 'new man' arise from the ashes of the 'old.'

The Christian has not done enough in this area of conversion to the neighbour, to social justice, to history. He has not perceived clearly enough yet that to know God *is* to do justice. He still does not live *in one sole action* with both God and all men. He still does not situate himself in Christ without attempting to avoid concrete human history. He has yet to tread the path which will lead him to seek effectively the peace of the Lord in the heart of the social struggle.

A spirituality of liberation must be filled with a living sense of *gratuitousness*. Communion with the Lord and with all men is more than anything else a gift. Hence the universality and the radicalness of the liberation which it affords. This gift, far from being a call to passivity, demands a vigilant attitude. This is one of the most constant Biblical themes: the encounter with the Lord presupposes attention, active disposition, work, fidelity to his will, the good use of talents received. But the knowledge that at the root of our personal and community existence lies the gift of the self-communication of God, the grace of his friendship, fills our life with gratitude. It allows us to see our encounters with men, our loves, everything that happens in our life as a gift. There is a real love only when there is free giving – without conditions or coercion. Only gratuitous love goes to our very roots and elicits true love.

Prayer is an experience of gratuitousness. This 'leisure' action, this 'wasted' time, reminds us that the Lord is beyond the categories of useful and useless. God is not of this world. The gratuitousness of his gift, creating profound needs, frees us from all religious alienation and, in the last instance, from all alienation. The Christian committed to the Latin American revolutionary process has to find the way to real prayer, not evasion. It cannot be denied that a crisis exists in this area and that we can easily slide into dead ends. There are many who – nostalgically and in 'exile,' recalling earlier years of their life – can say with the psalmist: 'As I pour out my soul in distress, I call to mind how I marched in the ranks of the great to the house of God, among exultant shouts of praise, the clamour of the pilgrims' (Ps. 42:4). But the point is not to backtrack; new experiences, new demands have made heretofore familiar and comfortable paths impassable and have made us undertake new itineraries on which we hope it might be possible to say with Job to the Lord, 'I knew thee then only by report, but now I see thee with my own eyes' (42:5). Bonhoeffer was right when he said that the only credible God is the God of the mystics. But this is not a God unrelated to human history. On the contrary, if it is true, as we recalled above, that one must go through man to reach God, it is equally certain that the 'passing through' to that gratuitous God strips me, leaves me naked, universalizes my love for others, and make it gratuitous. Both movements need each other dialectically and move towards a synthesis. This synthesis is found in Christ; in the God-Man we encounter God and man. In Christ man gives God a human countenance and God gives man a divine countenance. Only in this perspective will we be able to understand that the 'union with the Lord,' which all spirituality proclaims, is not a separation from man; to attain this union, I must go through man, and the union, in turn, enables me to encounter man more fully. Our purpose here is not to 'balance' what has been said before, but rather to deepen it and see it in all of its meaning.

The conversion to the neighbour, and in him to the Lord, the gratuitousness which allows me to encounter others fully, the unique encounter which is the foundation of communion of men among themselves and of men with God, these are the source of Christian *joy*. This joy is born of the gift already received yet still awaited and is expressed in the present despite the difficulties and tensions of the struggle for the construction of a just society. Every prophetic proclamation of total liberation is accompanied by an invitation to participate in eschatological joy: 'I will take delight in Jerusalem and rejoice in my people' (Isa 65:19). This joy ought to fill our entire existence, making us attentive both to the gift of integral liberation of man and history as well as to the detail of our life and the lives of others. This joy ought not to lessen our commitment to man who lives in an unjust world, nor should it lead us to a facile, low-cost conciliation. On the contrary, our joy is paschal, guaranteed by the Spirit (Gal. 5:22; 1 Tim. 1:6; Rom. 14:17); it passes through the conflict with the great ones of this world and through the cross in order to enter into life. This is why we celebrate our joy in the present by recalling the passover of the Lord. To recall Christ is to believe in him. And this celebration is a feast (Apoc. 19:7), a feast of the Christian community, those who explicitly confess Christ to be the Lord of history, the liberator of the oppressed. This community has been referred to as the small temple in contradistinction to the large temple of human history. Without community support neither the emergence nor the continued existence of a new spirituality is possible.

The Magnificat expresses well this spirituality of liberation. A song of thanksgiving for the gifts of the Lord, it expresses humbly the joy of being loved by him: 'Rejoice, my spirit, in God my Saviour; so tenderly has he looked upon his servant, humble as she is.... So wonderfully has he dealt with me, the Lord, the Mighty One' (Luke 1:47–49). But at the same time it is one of the New Testament texts which contains great implications both as regards liberation and the political sphere. This thanksgiving and joy are closely linked to the action of God who liberates the oppressed and humbles the powerful. 'The hungry he has satisfied with good things, the rich sent empty away' (52–53). The future of history belongs to the poor and exploited. True liberation will be the work of the oppressed themselves; in them, the Lord saves history. The spirituality of liberation will have as its basis the spirituality of the *anawim*.

Living witnesses rather than theological speculation will point out, are already pointing out, the direction of a spirituality of liberation. This is the task which has been undertaken in Latin America by those referred to above as a 'first Christian generation.'

Paulo Freire · *Education, Liberation and the Church*

Paulo Freire, 'Education, Liberation and the Church', *Study Encounter*, Vol. IX, No. 1, WCC 1973, pp.1-2, 12-16

We begin with an affirmation; though almost a truism, it clearly sets forth our position on the present subject. We cannot discuss churches, education or the role of the churches in education other than historically. Churches are not abstract entities, they are institutions involved in history. Therefore to understand their educational role we must take into consideration the concrete situation in which they exist.

The moment these statements are taken seriously, we can no longer speak of the neutrality of the churches or the neutrality of education. Such assertions of neutrality must be judged as coming either from those who have a totally naïve view of the church and history or from those who shrewdly mask a realistic understanding behind a claim of neutrality. Objectively, nevertheless, both groups fit into the same ideological perspective. When they insist on the neutrality of the church in relation to history, or to political action, they take political stands which inevitably favour the power elites against the masses. 'Washing one's hands' of the conflict between the powerful and the powerless means to side with the powerful, not to be neutral.

However, alongside the neutral attitude, there are more subtle and more attractive means of serving the interests of the powerful while appearing to favour the oppressed. Here again we find the 'naïve' and the 'shrewd' walking hand in hand. I refer to what we might call 'anaesthetic' or 'aspirin' practices, expressions of a subjectivist idealism that can only lead to the preservation of the status quo. In the last analysis the basic presupposition of such action is the illusion that the hearts of men and women can be transformed while the social structures which make those hearts 'sick' are left intact and unchanged.

The illusion which thinks it possible, by means of sermons, humanitarian works and the encouragement of other-worldly values, to change men's consciousness and thereby transform the world, exists only in those we term 'naïve' (or 'moralist' as Niebuhr would have said). The 'shrewd' are well aware that such action can slow down the basic process of radical change in social structures. This radical change is a precondition for the awakening of consciousness, and the process is neither automatic nor mechanical.

Although, objectively, both groups are equally ineffectual in producing liberation or the real humanization of human beings, there is still a basic difference between them which should be underlined. Both are caught up in the ideology of the ruling class but the shrewd consciously accept this ideology as their own. The naïve, in the first instance unconscious of their true position, can through their action come to take the ideology of domination for their own and, in the process, move from 'naïveness' to 'shrewdness'. They can also come to renounce their idealistic illusions altogether, forsaking their uncritical adherence to the ruling class. In committing themselves to the oppressed, they begin a new period of apprenticeship. This is not, however, to say that their commitment to the oppressed is thereby finally sealed. It will be severely tested during the course of this new apprenticeship when confronted, in a more serious and profound way than ever before, with the hazardous nature of existence. To win out in such a test is not easy.

This new apprenticeship will violently break down the elitist concept of existence which they had absorbed while being ideologized. The *sine qua non* which the apprenticeship demands is that, first of all, they really experience their own Easter, that they die as elitists so as to be resurrected on the side of the oppressed, that they be born again with the beings who were not allowed to be. Such a process implies a renunciation of myths which are dear to them: the myth of their 'superiority', of their purity of soul, of their virtues, their wisdom, the myth that they 'save the poor', the myth of the neutrality of the church, of theology, education, science, technology, the myth of their own impartiality – from which grow the other myths: of the inferiority of other people, of their spiritual and physical impurity, and the myth of the absolute ignorance of the oppressed.

This Easter, which results in the changing of consciousness, must be existentially experienced. The real Easter is not commemorative rhetoric. It is praxis; it is historical involvement. The old Easter of rhetoric is dead – with no hope of resurrection. It is only in the authenticity of historical praxis that Easter becomes the death which makes life possible. But the bourgeois world-view, basically necrophilic (death-loving) and therefore static is unable to accept this supremely biophilic (life-loving) experience of Easter. The bourgeois mentality – which is far more than just a convenient abstraction – kills the profound historical dynamism of Easter and turns it into no more than a date on the calendar.

The lust to possess, a sign of the necrophilic world-view, rejects the deeper meaning of resurrection. Why should I be interested in rebirth if I hold in my hands, as objects to be possessed, the torn body and soul of the oppressed? I can only experience rebirth at the side of the oppressed by being born again, with them, in the process of liberation. I cannot turn such a rebirth into a means of *owning* the world, since it is essentially a means of *transforming* the world.

If those who were once naïve continue their new apprenticeship, they will come to understand that consciousness is not changed by lessons, lectures and eloquent sermons but by the action of human beings on the world. Consciousness does not arbitrarily create reality, as they thought in their old naïve days of subjectivist idealism.

The Modernizing Church

We have seen that the modernization process of the dependent society never gets translated into fundamental changes in the relationship between the dependent society and the master society, and that the emergence of the masses does not by itself constitute their critical consciousness. In the same way, it is interesting to note, the churches' pilgrimage towards modernization never gets translated into historic involvement with the oppressed people in any real sense that leads towards that people's liberation.

Challenged by the increased efficiency of a society which is modernizing its archaic structures, the modernizing church improves its bureaucracy so that it can be more efficient in its social activities (its 'do-goodism') and in its pastoral activities. It replaces empirical means by technical processes. Its former 'charity centres' directed by lay persons (in the Catholic Church by the Daughters of Mary) become known as 'community centres', directed by social workers. And the men and women who were previously known by their own names are today numbers on a card index.

'Mass media' (which are actually media for issuing 'communiqués' to the masses), become an irresistible attraction to the churches. But the 'modern' and modernizing church can hardly be condemned for attempting to perfect its working tools; what is more serious is the political option which clearly conditions the process of modernization. Like the traditionalist churches, of which they are a new version, they are not committed to the oppressed but to the power elite. That is why they defend structural reform over against the radical transformation of structures; they speak of the 'humanization of capitalism' rather than its total suppression...

This is the kind of church which would still say to Christ today, 'Why leave, Master, if everything here is so beautiful, so good?' Their language conceals rather than reveals. It speaks of 'the poor' or of 'the underprivileged' rather than 'the oppressed'. While it sees the alienations of the ruling class and dominated class on the same level, it ignores the antagonism between them, the result of the system that created them. But, if the system alienates both groups, it alienates each in a different way. The rulers are alienated to the degree that, sacrificing their *being* for a false *having*, they are drugged with power and so stop *being*; the dominated, prevented to a certain degree from *having*, finish with so little power that *being* is impossible. Turning work into merchandise, the system creates those who buy it and those who sell it. The error of the naïve and the shrewdness of the shrewd is seen in their affirmation that such a contradiction is a purely moral question.

The ruling classes, as is the logic of the class system, prohibit the dominated class from *being*. In this process the ruling class itself ceases to *be*. The system itself keeps them from rising above the contradiction, from any movement which would end their alienation as well as that of those they dominate. The dominated alone are called to fulfil this task in history. The ruling class, as such, cannot carry it out. What they can do – within their historical limits – is to reform and to modernize the system according to the new demands which the system allows them to perceive, thus in effect maintaining that which results in the alienation of all.

Under the conditions in which the modernizing churches act, their concepts of education, its objectives, its application, all must form a coherent unity within their general political position. That is why, even though they speak of liberating education, they are conditioned by their vision of liberation as an individual activity which should take place through a change of consciousness and not through the social and historical praxis of human beings. So they end up by putting the accent on methods which can be considered neutral. Liberating education for the modernizing church is finally reduced to liberating the students from blackboards, static classes and text-book curricula, and offering them projectors and other audio-visual accessories, more dynamic classes and a new technico-professional teaching.

The Prophetic Church

Finally, another kind of church has been taking shape in Latin America, though it is not often visible as a coherent totality. It is a church as old as Christianity itself, without being traditional; as new as Christianity, without being modernizing. It is the prophetic church. Opposed and attacked by both traditionalist and modernizing churches, as well as by the elite of the power structures, this utopian, prophetic and hope-filled movement rejects do-goodism and palliative reforms in order to commit itself to the dominated social classes and to radical social change.

In contrast with the churches considered above, it rejects all static forms of thought. It accepts becoming, in order to *be*. Because it thinks critically this prophetic church cannot think of itself as neutral. Nor does it try to hide its choice. Therefore it does not separate worldliness from transcendence or salvation from liberation. It knows that what finally counts is not the 'I am' or the 'I know'; the 'I free myself' or the 'I save myself'; nor even the 'I teach you', 'I free you', or 'I save you', but the 'we are', 'we know', 'we save ourselves'.

This prophetic line can only be understood as an expression of the dramatic and challenging situation of Latin America. It emerges when the contradictions in Latin American society become apparent. It is at this moment, too, that revolution is seen as the means of liberation for the oppressed people, and the military coup as the reactionary counter-move.

Latin America's 'prophetic' Christians may disagree among themselves, especially at the point of 'action', but they are the ones who have renounced their innocence in order to join the oppressed classes, and who remain faithful to their commitment. Protestant or Catholic – from the point of view of this prophetic position the division is of no importance – clergy or lay, they have all had to travel a hard route of experience from their idealistic visions towards a dialectical vision of reality. They have learned, not only as a result of their praxis with the people, but also from the courageous example of many young people. They now see that reality, a process and not a static fact, is full of contradictions, and that social conflicts are not metaphysical categories but rather historical expressions of the confrontation of these contradictions.

Any attempt, therefore, to solve conflict without touching the contradictions which have generated it only stifles the conflict and at
the same time strengthens the ruling class.

The prophetic position demands a critical analysis of the social
structures in which the conflict takes place. This means that it
demands of its followers a knowledge of socio-political science,
since this science cannot be neutral; this demands an ideological
choice.

Such prophetic perspective does not represent an escape into a
world of unattainable dreams. It demands a scientific knowledge
of the world as it really is. For to denounce the present reality and
announce its radical transformation into another reality capable
of giving birth to new men and women, implies gaining through
praxis a new knowledge of reality. The dominated classes must
take part in this denunciation and annunciation. It cannot be done
if they are left out of the picture. The prophetic position is not
petit bourgeois. It is well aware that authentic action demands a
permanent process which only reaches its maximal point when
the dominated class, through praxis, also becomes prophetic,
utopian and full of hope – in other words, revolutionary. A society
in a state of permanent revolution cannot manage without a
permanent prophetic vision. Without it, society stagnates and is
no longer revolutionary.

In the same way, no church can be really prophetic if it remains
the 'haven of the masses' or the agent of modernization and con-
servation. The prophetic church is no home for the oppressed,
alienating them further by empty denunciations. On the contrary,
it invites them to a new Exodus. Nor is the prophetic church one
which chooses modernization and thereby does no more than
stagnate. Christ was no conservative. The prophetic church, like
Him, must move forward constantly, forever dying and forever
being reborn. In order to be, it must always be in a state of *becoming*. The prophetic church must also accept an existence which is
in dramatic tension between past and future, staying and going,
speaking the Word and keeping silence, being and not being.
There is no prophecy without risk.

This prophetic attitude, which emerges in the praxis of numerous
Christians in the challenging historical situation of Latin America,
is accompanied by a rich and very necessary theological reflection.
The theology of so-called development gives way to the theology
of liberation – a prophetic, utopian theology, full of hope. Little
does it matter that this theology is not yet well systematized. Its
content arises from the hopeless situation of dependent, exploited,

invaded societies. It is stimulated by the need to rise above the contradictions which explain and produce that dependence. Since it is prophetic, this theology of liberation cannot attempt to reconcile the irreconcilable ...

Europeans and North Americans, with their technological societies, have no need to go to Latin America in order to become prophetic. They need only go to the outskirts of their big cities, without 'naiveté' or 'shrewdness', and there they will find sufficient stimulus to do some fresh thinking for themselves. They will find themselves confronted with various expressions of the Third World. They can begin to understand the concern which gives rise to the prophetic position in Latin America.

Thus it is clear that the educational role of the prophetic church in Latin America must be totally different from that of the other churches we have discussed. Education must be an instrument of transforming action, as a political praxis at the service of permanent human liberation. This, let us repeat, does not happen only in the consciousness of people, but presupposes a radical change of structures, in which process consciousness will itself be transformed.

From the prophetic point of view, it makes little difference in what specific area education happens, it will always be an effort to clarify the concrete context in which the teacher-students and student-teachers are educated and are united by their presence in action. It will always be a demythologizing praxis.

Which brings us back to our opening statement: the Church, education and the role of the churches in education can only be discussed historically. It is in history that mankind is called to respond to the prophetic movement in Latin America.

Hugo Assmann · *Basic Aspects of Theological Reflection in Latin America*

Hugo Assmann, 'Basic Aspects of Theological Reflection in Latin America: a critical evaluation of the "Theology of Liberation"', *Risk*, Vol. 9, No. 2, WCC 1973, pp.26-33

The mythologizing of Latin American theology bothers me because it implies a distortion of the facts

I think that the attention being paid to the supposed 'boom' in

Latin American theology is not only out of proportion: it is distorting.

The so-called Theology of Liberation has acquired mythical proportions. According to my very incomplete knowledge – there are five theological theses being written on this subject, four extensive bibliographies which have the merit of spelling out the repercussions and symptomatic reactions, an enormous amount of reviews and short bibliographies, etc.

In my judgment, the most important distortions are not those of an inquisitorial character – heresy hunting – because they reveal themselves with sufficient clarity (for example, cables datelined *Rome* which credit the 'theologians of liberation' with absurd positions on subjects upon which they have not taken a stand because they are not priority subjects in Latin America but rather are important to the Rich World [for example, celibacy, abortion, contraception, anti-ecclesiastical aggressiveness . . .].

There is an even greater distortion in this sort of mythologizing: in the consideration of texts the analysis does not include the situational context which gave rise to them as historical instruments of struggle. Therefore, what appears in these writings as an essential reference of origin and finality passes on to a secondary level. And so, once more, it is confirmed that idealism feeds on what was meant to be an irradication of theological idealism. Perhaps a theology of hope is an idealistic digression.

It is not necessary to go into the danger of a recuperative draining of new languages so clearly present in this phenomenon and the advantages this drainage brings to the system.

In Latin America many theologians are beginning to question this drainage of language and are exposing their own guilt with the rapid expansion of the integrated languages of the system. That little word *liberation* today covers everything imaginable, from the most individual and intimate experiences, through the mythology of the marginal groups which exclude themselves from real history, to the collective processes of diverse brands of ideology. Whatever happened to the analytical, narrow, well-defined political option which from the beginning presided over the language and clothed the anti-system praxis, in the case of Theology of Liberation? It would seem that Christians have a great capacity to create new languages – initially provocative, quickly emptied, and, finally, perfectly integrated – serving as a formidable 'experience in limits' as a test of the soundness of the structures being challenged . . .

Given this remarkable confusion of languages with respect to the theology of liberation, it is perhaps important not to forget that when more relevant things are happening in the life of the people than are happening (or rather, not happening) in theology, it is a good sign that the testimonies – fragmentary, provisional, without abstract theoretical consistency – have a theological resonance greater than that of theological treatises. Perhaps the positive aspect of the enormous repercussion of our Christian babbling in Latin America is this very point: the testimonial offered by the commitment to a decided struggle against capitalistic oppression. If this is what has awakened a certain interest, it is good. It states clearly: Don't take our writings for something which they are not; don't transform us into a consumer product to make up for your impotence; don't be spectators of our small achievements, nor project on Latin America an image of compensations; and finally, all of you, each in his own context, enter into the same struggle . . .

Faced with the importance of all this, what I feel I must add to the motivation for this dialogue becomes secondary.

Some more thoughts on the recent stages of reflection by revolutionary Christians in Latin America

I would like to abandon, at this point, the broad generality which could have remained the basis of my original title. I will refer now to those Christian areas which have taken a defined revolutionary stand. This is my context because this is my experience. Having chosen the limited context of revolutionary Christianity, it is important to eliminate certain inaccuracies. First of all, we are not talking about all of the churches in Latin America. This must be said openly in order, once and for all, to stop this 'numbers game' of committed groups. The committed groups are, in fact, minority groups within their churches. It is the relevance of their quality – and little by little their quantity – which makes them strongly felt within their churches. But quite frankly, they *are* a minority and are extremely conscious of their minority status.

Also a tremendous influx of foreign capital has been channelled through the churches into Latin America outside the 'committed groups', the World Council of Churches and German agencies, to name two examples.

Presently, with variations from country to country, there are a number of conflicts, but there is also a widening tolerance. However, this sort of detailed analysis must be done country by country. Since that is impossible here, let us look at the over-all picture.

There is at present a clear retreat within the hierarchical levels of the churches – even in CELAM (Latin American Episcopal Conference) – which calls for analysis on an international level. There is an exhaustion of energy supplies among the pastoral-style reformists. The importing of progressive theologies from the cities, however, has sharply diminished in recent years, since the bone marrow of these theologies has become visible; many sectors of the clergy, of pastors, of Christian intellectuals, and even some popular sectors, find themselves in a complicated phase in which they are building their religious independence.

This creation of a Christianity with Latin American roots is still in the early stages and is being channelled for the most part into political positions, to the point where I can say that politics today is the essential road for Christian consciousness, almost equally so for the left and for the right. The class struggle is becoming more acute within the churches as it becomes more acute in society. With all of this, for the majority of Christian revolutionaries open confrontation with their churches is an unacceptable political thesis because it causes a fatal confusion between the relevancies of 'the enemies'. Their efforts to maintain good relations with the church hierarchy are not a simple, opportunist tactic, but rather represent a mature analysis of what Christianity means historically as a mass religion in Latin America. It can even be said that a new awareness of church membership is emerging for historical reasons which are becoming theologically concrete ...

At this level of broad strategy there remain many questions about the concrete basis of faith and of politics for revolutionary Christians. Almost all of the questions raised in the theology of liberation are at this level.

Some examples :

– the rejection of 'developmentism' in social analysis;
– Christian mediating reactions: dependence-liberation;
– the need for a collection of practical theoretical mediations in reflections on faith;
– the re-definition of theology as a 'critical reflection on the situation';
– the tie between theology and social sciences;
– the overcoming of the false scheme of church-world;
– the reception of the Marxist position on social reality and its interpretation;
– the basic option for socialism as expressed in the First Latin American Meeting of Christians for Socialism;

– the affirmation of the historical class struggle as fact and as method.

What is of interest here is not so much thematic analysis which is determined by how this level of strategy-in-the-broad-sense is reached (for example, how a profoundly new and impressive theology of sin came about), but rather to underline the importance of what took place at this level.

To summarize: what is basic can be seen in these examples:

– re-definition of the subject of theology – no longer the domain of the individual theologian but rather of a politically committed group;
– the replacement of the central objective of theology from 'thinking' to praxis;
– complete re-thinking about the instruments of theological reflection which gives a sense of 'now' to the Word of God;
– the discovery of the liberal and intra-system substance of the progressive theologies of the Rich World;
– the connection between 'intra-ecclesiastical reformism' and 'modernization of the socio-economic sense';
– an admission of the provisional aspect of theological reflection;
– a new freedom to use the Bible as a resource without discarding exegetical advances, and at the same time, without accepting their customary liberal ideological framework and their digression to themes without great historical relevance.

It is clear to those who have analysed the enormous quantity of writings which have been labelled expressions of the theology of liberation, that progress has varied through the different stages – some slower, some more rapid, some more explicit here, some more explicit there, and so on.

Given its symptomatic importance, the increasingly coherent explicitness of socialism and the successive confrontation of the class struggle (tabu for the majority of Christians) can be seen as leads in the evolution of the broad strategy.

The situational sub-strategies in projects of national liberation

The framework of the broad strategy is insufficient for an understanding of Christian reflection in the different Latin American countries. A much more detailed analysis is necessary if you are to understand the situation and language of committed Christians in Latin America.

At this level the matter becomes more complex. As it is not possible here to make a detailed analysis, I will re-state the fact – scandalous to those who continue to fool themselves and others with the myth of 'pure theology' – that, for example, the writings of Lucio Gera, Argentina's best-known theologian, and his group cannot be understood without an understanding of their sub-strategy of national liberation in the light of Peronism. Without this context, his presentation of the theological question of 'the children of God' with its vital reference to the Argentinian cause cannot be understood. Further, without an understanding of the sub-strategies, the different variations of the tools of Marxist analysis cannot be understood. The option for socialism, and within the Christian option, can only be defined within the framework of the sub-strategies – often contradictory – within the same leftist positions which are not necessarily antagonistic, in the fertile dialectic of the chosen road to socialism. This is reflected in the mediations which make up the language of faith.

The two levels – over-all strategy and sub-strategy – are not fighting with each other on basic issues but, instead, are complementary. However, they can appear to be using quite different languages in any given situation.

The decision centres of ecclesiastical institutions are well aware of this fact and keep it very much in mind. Again, it is necessary to analyse the unconscious ideological functions behind the generalized resistance of 'theologians' (the professionals) in order to reach the strategic-tactical level. Without this historical understanding, it is an abstraction.

Even more strange is the proliferation of theological theses which allude to these fundamentals.

A hypothesis acting as a certainty at the subjective level in the conscience of some Latin American Christians

To conclude, I want to mention a basic hypothesis which I have observed not only in my contacts with theologians and groups dedicated to a Christian revolutionary reflection, but also in popular groups: that the specific mission of our continent is the hard task of 'Christianization'.

All over the world, historical Christianity has lost its prophetic dimension and is an enslaved Church. How can we re-think it in order to recover its domesticated energies?

Latin America – as a Third-World Christian package – will, perhaps, have to give the universal Church a small push towards its re-Christianization.

There are several factors in this hypothesis:

- theology goes no further than reform in the Rich World;
- the churches are experiencing a crisis which is only secondarily doctrinal: a crisis which demands an analysis of historical Christianity with reference to over-all strategies;
- theological heresies have become irrelevant in the Rich World (the Dutch Catholic reform does not interest Latin America: in Brazil the New Dutch Catechism appears with the full support of a repressive government);
- the role played by religious acts as a social factor in the Third World is quite different from their role in the developed world;
- in Latin America the churches are not in conflict with Marxism (and are even more revolutionary than 'domesticated' Marxism) but at the same time they do not feed hegemonic pretentions *à la Constantine* and the new version of secularization to its people;
- in this prophetic doctrinaire, the dogmatic which is the source and support of institutional ideologies undergoes practical criticism (for example, when the theology regarding the 'apostolic succession' and the 'historical representatives of Christ' was forced to confront the weight of Christian political representatives);
- the subject of 'Faith and Politics' is forced into an historical and social encounter, including the subject of 'Religion and Politics';
- dialogue is activated within the churches without their becoming underground churches, or anti-ecclesiastical;
- the Christian-Marxist dialogue – having overcome the theoretical flirtation of the '60s – is making a qualitative jump towards fellowship in the struggle.

I have quite a few reservations about this hypothesis. Until recently, similar attempts at social prophecy throughout the history of the Church – especially Christian socialism – have always been crushed by ecclesiastical institutions. In addition, what is happening in Latin America is not yet a reality, although its vigour and solidarity are growing. Perhaps even more prophets must die in order to awaken the churches. There are those who accept this perspective of Latin America, which says a great deal about their love of the Church. There are also those naïve ones who expect an early re-dialectization of historical Christianity, which does not seem likely to me.

Anyway, the hypothesis is full of challenges ...

6 · Black Theology

In discussing theology of development it was noted that the world is divided into rich and poor nations, developed and underdeveloped and that this division might also be expressed as the white north against the black south. In this context 'black' is used in a peculiar way. It does not refer simply to colour, indeed it hardly concerns colour at all. It is used indiscriminately and certainly without offensiveness to refer to people whose experience, consciousness and situation is in starkest contrast to the white north, especially the West. In this widest sense of the term therefore 'black' theology might be the theology arising from the experience of Christians in the Third World. In fact the phrase applies in the first instance to the theology which comes from the black community within the USA. In so far as the black community there is part of the Third World *within* America there are affinities between black theology and theology of liberation. (This was made clear at the theological symposium in Geneva, May 1973 on 'Black Theology and Latin American Theology of Liberation'.)

Black theology arises from the experience of black Christians in America, especially as they were caught up in the political sequence which began with the civil rights movement of the late 1950s and early 1960s. When we remember the long tradition of segregation in America, especially in the South but also throughout the North, and the brutal way in which the whites dealt with any 'niggers' who stepped out of line nothing must detract from the courage of those who, with actions such as that of Rosa Parks in Montgomery in 1955, led the movements towards the recognition of civil rights for all citizens. But this first stage in the movement was in a sense a re-enforcement of white racialism. It was a movement to achieve for negroes (as they were then called) what belonged to whites. The goal was integration. There is a strange parallel here with what was said in the discussion of the development debate. Like the underdeveloped countries at the same period of history, the negro community took white society as their goal. They wanted to be like the white community. The civil rights movement did not lessen the practice of hair-straightening or the sale of lotions to lighten the colour of the skin. The negro community was still under the influence of the whites: the dominant ideas, customs and values were those of the dominant community.

But as in the development debate, ironically, dependence was finally broken when it was demonstrated by the rich countries that the gap between the two groups was not going to be eliminated or even threatened, so the greatest advance among blacks was made when the white community in America made it very clear that blacks would not be fully accepted. As long as civil rights were being gradually accorded moderation seemed reasonable and justified. But what more could the civil rights campaign achieve than the March on Washington and the passing of the Civil Rights Bill of 1964? When, two years later, the goal of equality was no nearer the black community became increasingly disenchanted with the moderate leadership of Martin Luther King. By the time of his assassination in 1968 the initiative had moved to more radical leaders.

To pursue the parallel with the development debate, in which the closing of the door to development led to a reappraisal of such goals in any case, the denial of equality and integration led to a questioning of these objectives. And more importantly, the experience of the closed door led to a raising of consciousness in the Third World about their real situation. So now the blacks, denied equality with whites, began to understand the realities of their situation as for the first time, and were forced to take a long look at themselves. As in the liberation theology, the dominant fact of black life emerged as dependence – economic, cultural and even to some extent spiritual. From 1966 the goal was to end such dependence. For convenience the movement can be seen as Black Power and Black Consciousness, though there was no division in reality.

As early as 1965, the Rev. Adam Clayton Powell, New York Congressman, was using the phrase 'black power' to draw attention to the fact that the black community must control the circumstances and institutions of their own lives. The phrase was converted into a slogan by Stokely Carmichael in Mississippi the following year. Even more dramatic was the formation of the Black Panther Party, also in 1966, by Huey Newton and Bobby Seale. They saw the growth of interest in blackness as a possible distraction, and opposed the 'cultural nationalists'. They drew up a specific programme of demands concerned with employment, housing, education, welfare, fair treatment by the police and justice in the courts. The outlawing of segregated education and the passing of a bill on civil rights had underlined the fact that until the Second World War it had not occurred to Americans generally that the American Constitution might also apply to blacks. So it was with a rare and ironic sense of humour that the Panthers started to carry firearms under that Amendment so beloved of the gun lobby in Washington, which gives the right to all Americans to carry arms.

The sight of blacks doing what whites had done for centuries sent waves of fear and dismay across the nation, and confirmed – if confirmation were required – that the white community still had not come to terms with equality for blacks. The Panthers were rejected out of hand, as if somehow they had introduced racialism into America for the first time. But although racialism has always been part of American society, Marxism and socialism have not. It was interesting, therefore, to hear that the Panthers saw their struggle in quite different terms from those who sought to destroy them. In *Seize the Time* Bobby Seale declares: 'We, the Black Panther Party, see ourselves as a nation within a nation, but not for any racist reasons. We see it as a necessity for us to progress as human beings and live on the face of the earth along with other people. We do not fight racism with racism. We fight racism with solidarity. We do not fight exploitative capitalism with black capitalism. We fight capitalism with basic socialism.' Or more briefly, 'we believe our fight is a class struggle and not a race struggle.'

The black community seemed to require a dramatic representation of the need to end dependence at all levels. It is to the shame of American history that this symbol was the gun. And although the guns were used on occasion they symbolized the beginnings of a black exodus from the place that had been assigned to blacks within a white society. The most important contribution was to allow black consciousness to develop. The affirmation of blackness in the modern world is associated with what Aimé Césaire called 'negritude'. Fanon, once again, was influential in analysing how able blacks were increasingly accepted in white society so long as they became white. But within America the militant affirmation of blackness and the corresponding rejection of everything white cannot be dissociated from black nationalism and The Honourable Elijah Muhammed. The Black Muslims, the Nation of Islam, began to attract widespread interest from about 1960. Malcolm Little was converted to the faith while in prison. The year following his release Malcolm X was appointed Assistant Minister to Temple Number One in Detroit. He constantly spoke out against white society, white religion and encouraged blacks to have nothing to do with the white man, the white devil. It must be said that in the ghettos of America he gave new heart and self-respect to thousands of black people who had been made marginals within their own country. He contributed a great deal to the emergent black consciousness which began wherever dependence on the white community was challenged. Following his suspension by Elijah Muhammed in 1964 he moved to establish closer links with other religious leaders equally concerned with black militancy and then finally, before his assassination in 1965, he formed the Organization of Afro-American Unity.

It will be clear, therefore, that black theology is not simply a result of black theologians speaking out of their American religious heritage. Their heritage now is of black power, the riots of Watts and Newark and militant black religion. They now belong to a culture which is Afro-American. To be a Christian in a negro community was quite normal: to be a Christian in such a culture which is suspicious of all white infiltration is another matter. Christianity has strong associations with slave religion and slave mentality, a religion of consolation which made tolerable an intolerable world. In fairness it must be said that this was not the whole story. Gayraud Wilmore has traced in *Black Religion and Black Radicalism* the rise of the black churches, from the last quarter of the eighteenth century and the early associations of black consciousness with a turning towards Africa. There was Andrew Bryan in 1788 at the first African Baptist Church in Savannah, Richard Allen in the previous year founding the Free African Society in Philadelphia and Robert Alexander Young's 'The Ethiopian Manifesto', published in New York in 1829; there was Edward Blyden's emigration to Liberia and his *Christianity, Islam and the Negro Race*, sometimes referred to as the first attempt to write theology from a black perspective.

Even so, black theology comes from a situation created largely by factors outside the Christian Church and often hostile to Christianity as the religion of the white man and the uncle Tom. Thus in 1966 when white America, including the white churches, was alarmed at the growth of support for the idea of black power, the National Committee of Negro Churchmen published a statement indicating why the call for black power had come about. The following year saw a conference organized by the National Council of Churches in Washington at which the black delegates insisted on dividing the conference into two caucuses – black and white. Dependence within the churches has now been challenged.

For those who are aware of the assimilation of Christianity and Western (white) culture and who wish to find some way of distancing the one from the other, the most exciting thing about black theology is that it springs from another cultural setting altogether. But in so far as the experience of the black community is one of oppression, injustice, suffering and powerlessness then there is the possibility that this experience may lead to a truer appreciation of the gospel than is possible for those who live in a society that is affluent and exercises power in the world at large. Almost inevitably there tends to be a strident militancy about black theology – or black theologians – and the Christian element seems almost subordinated to a general black religious assertiveness. For example there is the Rev. Albert Cleage of the Shrine of the Black Madonna, Detroit, and the sentiments expressed in his collected sermons, *The Black Messiah*. But there are other themes which may be more central to the contribution of black theology to the white churches, such as powerlessness and the cross, suffering and reconciliation.

Finally, we began by noting that black theology in its widest sense might be the theology of the Third World. Not surprisingly black theology has begun to emerge in South Africa, and although it is still to a large extent influenced by the American expression, it should eventually take a quite distinct form corresponding to the distinct experience of blacks in South Africa. The All Africa Council of Churches arranged a conference in Nairobi this year on 'Black and African Theologies'. The older forms of theology have stemmed largely from the initiatives of European anthropologists who have encouraged Africans to look to their cultural heritage in the past. The new form of African theology springs from a new consciousness among Africans of their political situation and far from being about the past, is oriented towards the future.

James H. Cone · *The Gospel of Jesus, Black People, and Black Power*

James H. Cone, *Black Theology and Black Power*, Seabury Press, NY 1969, pp.31-40, 42-43, 52-54, 60-61. © 1969 by The Seabury Press, Inc. Used by permission

Contemporary theology from Karl Barth to Jürgen Moltmann conceives of the theological task as one which speaks from within the covenant community with the sole purpose of making the gospel meaningful to the times in which men live. While the gospel itself does not change, every generation is confronted with new problems, and the gospel must be brought to bear on them. Thus, the task of theology is to show what the changeless gospel means in each new situation.

On the American scene today, as yesterday, one problem stands out: the enslavement of black Americans. But as we examine what contemporary theologians are saying, we find that they are silent about the enslaved condition of black people. Evidently they see no relationship between black slavery and the Christian gospel. Consequently there has been no sharp confrontation of the gospel and white racism. There is, then, a desperate need for a *black theology*, a theology whose sole purpose is to apply the freeing power of the gospel to black people under white oppression.

In more sophisticated terms this may be called a theology of revolution. Lately there has been much talk about revolutionary theology, stemming primarily from non-Western religious thinkers whose identification lies with the indigenous oppressed people of the land. These new theologians of the 'Third World' argue that Christians should not shun violence but should initiate it, if violence is the only means of achieving the much needed rapid radical changes in life under dehumanizing systems. They are not confident, as most theologians from industrialized nations seem to be, that changes in the economic structure (from agrarian to industrial) of a country will lead to changes in its oppressive power-structure. (America seems to be the best indication that they are probably correct.) Therefore their first priority is to change the structures of power.

The present work seeks to be revolutionary in the sense that it attempts to bring to theology a special attitude permeated with black consciousness. It asks the question, What does the Christian gospel have to say to powerless black men whose existence is threatened daily by the insidious tentacles of white power? Is there a message from Christ to the countless number of blacks whose lives are smothered under white society? Unless theology can become 'ghetto theology,' a theology which speaks to black people, the gospel message has no promise of life for the black man – it is a lifeless message. Unfortunately, even black theologians have, more often than not, merely accepted the problems defined by white theologians. Their treatment of Christianity has been shaped by the dominant ethos of the culture. There have been very few, if any, radical, revolutionary approaches to the Christian gospel for oppressed blacks. There is, then, a need for a theology whose sole purpose is to emancipate the gospel from its 'whiteness' so that blacks may be capable of making an honest self-affirmation through Jesus Christ.

This work further seeks to be revolutionary in that 'The fact that I am Black is my ultimate reality' (Maulana Ron Karenga). My identity with *blackness*, and what it means for millions living in a white world, controls the investigation. It is impossible for me to surrender this basic reality for a 'higher, more universal' reality. Therefore, if a higher, Ultimate Reality is to have meaning, it must relate to the very essence of blackness. Certainly, white Western Christianity with its emphasis on individualism and capitalism as expressed in American Protestantism is unreal for blacks. And if Christianity is not real for blacks who are seeking black consciousness through the elements of Black Power, then they will reject it.

Unfortunately, Christianity came to the black man through white oppressors who demanded that he reject his concern for this world as well as his blackness and affirm the next world and whiteness. The black intellectual community, however, with its emphasis on black identity, is becoming increasingly suspicious of Christianity because the oppressor has used it as a means of stifling the oppressed concern for present inequities. Naturally, as the slave questions his existence as a slave, he also questions the religion of the enslaver. 'We must,' writes Maulana Ron Karenga, 'concern ourselves more with this life which has its own problems. For the next life across Jordan is much further away from the growl of dogs and policemen and the pains of hunger and disease.'

Therefore, it is appropriate to ask: Is it possible for men to be *really* black and still feel any identity with the biblical tradition expressed in the Old and the New Testaments? Is it possible to strip the gospel as it has been interpreted of its 'whiteness,' so that its real message will become a live option for radical advocates of black consciousness? Is there any relationship at all between the work of God and the activity of the ghetto? Must black people be forced to deny their identity in order to embrace the Christian faith? Finally, is Black Power, as described in Chapter I, compatible with the Christian faith, or are we dealing with two utterly divergent perspectives? These are hard questions. To answer these questions, however, we need to discuss, first, the gospel of Jesus as it relates to black people ...

If the gospel is a gospel of liberation for the oppressed, then Jesus is where the oppressed are and continues his work of liberation there. Jesus is not safely confined in the first century. He is our contemporary, proclaiming release to the captives and rebelling against all who silently accept the structures of injustice. If he is not in the ghetto, if he is not where men are living at the brink of existence, but is, rather, in the easy life of the suburbs, then the gospel is a lie. The opposite, however, is the case. Christianity is not alien to Black Power; it is Black Power.

There are secular interpretations which attempt to account for present black rebellion, as there have been secular interpretations of the exodus or of the life and death of Jesus. But for the Christian, there is only one interpretation: Black rebellion is a manifestation of God himself actively involved in the present-day affairs of men for the purpose of liberating a people. Through his work, black people now know that there is something more important than life itself. They can afford to be indifferent towards death, because life devoid of freedom is not worth living. They can now sing with a sense of triumph, 'Oh, Freedom! Oh, Freedom! Oh Freedom over me! An' befo' I'd be a slave, I'd be buried in my grave, an' go home to my Lord an' be free.'

Christ, Black Power, and Freedom

An even more radical understanding of the relationship of the gospel to Black Power is found in the concept of freedom. We have seen that freedom stands at the centre of the black man's yearning in America. 'Freedom Now' has been and still is the echoing slogan of all civil rights groups. The same concept of freedom is presently expressed among Black Power advocates by such phrases as 'self-determination' and 'self-identity.'

What is this freedom for which blacks have marched, boycotted, picketed, and rebelled in order to achieve? Simply stated, freedom is *not doing what I will but becoming what I should. A man is free when he sees clearly the fulfilment of his being and is thus capable of making the envisioned self a reality.* This is 'Black Power!' They want the grip of white power removed. This is what black people have in mind when they cry, 'Freedom Now!' now and forever.

Is this not why God became man in Jesus Christ so that man might become what he is? Is not this at least a part of what St. Paul had in mind when he said, 'For freedom, Christ has set us free' (Gal. 5:1)? As long as man is a slave to another power, he is not free to serve God with mature responsibility. He is not free to become what he is – human.

Freedom is indeed what distinguishes man from animals and plants. 'In the case of animals and plants nature not only appoints the destiny but it alone carries it out.... In the case of man, however, nature provides only the destiny and leaves it to him to carry it out' (H. Thielicke). Black Power means black people carrying out their own destiny.

It would seem that Black Power and Christianity have this in common: the liberation of man! If the work of Christ is that of liberating men from alien loyalties, and if racism is, as George Kelsey says, an alien faith, then there must be some correlation between Black Power and Christianity. For the gospel proclaims that God is with us now, actively fighting the forces which would make man captive. And it is the task of theology and the Church to know where God is at work so that we can join him in this fight against evil. In America we know where the evil is. We know that men are shot and lynched. We know that men are crammed into ghettos. Black Power is the power to say No; it is the power of blacks to refuse to cooperate in their own dehumanization. If blacks can trust the message of Christ, if they take him at his word, this power to say No to white power and domination is derived from him.

With reference, then, to freedom in Christ, three assertions about Black Power can be made: First, the work of Christ is essentially a liberating work, directed toward and by the oppressed. Black Power embraces that very task. Second, Christ in liberating the wretched of the earth also liberates those responsible for the wretchedness. The oppressor is also freed of his peculiar demons. Black Power in shouting Yes to black humanness and No to white oppression is exorcising demons on both sides of the conflict. Third, mature freedom is burdensome and risky, producing anxiety and

conflict for free men and for the brittle structures they challenge.
The call for Black Power is precisely the call to shoulder the burden
of liberty in Christ, risking everything to live not as slaves but as
free men.

With this interpretation in view, we now ask: What does this
mean to the black man in America today? What does it mean to
speak of God's love to man? Man's response to God? His love
of neighbour?

For God to love the black man means that God has made him
somebody. The black man does not need to hate himself because
he is not white, and he should feel no need to become like others.
His blackness, which society despises, is a special creation of God
himself. He has worth because God imparts value through loving.
It means that God has bestowed on him a new image of himself,
so that he can now become what he in fact is. Through God's love,
the black man is given the power to *become*, the power to make
others recognize him. Because God is 'a God of power; of majesty
and of might,' to love man means that he wills that the black man
'reflect in the immediacies of life his power, his majesty and his
might' (N. Wright).

For the black man to respond to God's love in faith means that
he accepts as truth the new image of himself revealed in Jesus
Christ. He now knows that the definition of himself defined by
white society is inconsistent with the newly found image disclosed
in Christ. In a world which has taught blacks to hate themselves,
the new black man does not transcend blackness, but accepts it,
loves it as a gift of the Creator. For he knows that until he accepts
himself as a being of God in all of its physical blackness, he can
love neither God nor neighbour. This may be what one Black
Power advocate meant when he said: 'Until blacks develop themselves, they can do nothing for humanity.' And another who said,
'Black Power does not teach hatred; it teaches love. But it teaches
us that love, like charity, must begin at home; that it must begin
with ourselves, our beautiful black selves.'

When St. Paul speaks of being 'a new creature' in Christ, the
redeemed black man takes that literally. He glorifies blackness,
not as a means of glorifying self in the egotistical sense, but merely
as an acceptance of the black self as a creature of God.

But what does it mean for the black man to love the neighbour,
especially the white neighbour? To love the white man means
that the black man *confronts* him as a Thou without any intentions of giving ground by becoming an It. Though the white man

is accustomed to addressing an It, in the new black man he meets a Thou. The black man must, if he is not to lose sight of his new-found identity in Christ, be prepared for conflict, for a radical confrontation. As one black man put it: 'Profound love can only exist between two equals.' The new black man refuses to assume the It-role which whites expect, but addresses them as an equal. This is when the conflict arises.

Therefore the new black man refuses to speak of love without justice and power. Love without the power to guarantee justice in human relations is meaningless. Indeed, there is no place in Christian theology for sentimental love, love without risk or cost. Love demands all, the whole of one's being. Thus, for the black man to believe the Word of God about his love revealed in Christ, he must be prepared to meet head-on the sentimental 'Christian' love of whites, which would make him a nonperson.

Black Power, though not consciously seeking to be Christian, seems to be where men are in trouble. And to the extent that it is genuinely concerned and seeks to meet the needs of the oppressed, it is the work of God's Spirit. By contrast the self-consciously 'Christian' person so easily uses the poor as a means to his own salvation. But unless the condition of the poor becomes the condition of the Christian, not because he feels sorry for the poor, but because through the Spirit of Christ he is in fact poor, all acts done on behalf of them are nothing in the eyes of God ...

Black Power, then, is God's new way of acting in America. It is his way of saying to blacks that they are human beings; he is saying to whites: 'Get used to it!'

Whites, as well as some blacks, will find the encounter of Black Power a terrible experience. Like the people of Jesus' day, they will find it hard to believe that God would stoop so low as to reveal himself in and through black people and especially the 'undesirable elements.' If he has to make himself known through blacks, why not choose the 'good Negroes'? But, that is just the point: God encounters men at that level of experience which challenges their being. The real test of whether whites can communicate with blacks as human beings is not what they reply to Ralph Bunche but how they respond to Rap Brown.

Gayraud S. Wilmore · *Black Power, Black People, Theological Renewal*

Gayraud S. Wilmore, *Black Religion and Black Radicalism*, Doubleday, NY 1972, pp.298-306. © 1972 by Gayraud S. Wilmore. Used by permission of Doubleday Company Inc.

The first source of Black theology is in the existing Black community, where the tradition of Black folk religion is still extant and continues to stand over against the institutional church – merging with it at times in the ministry of such men as Henry M. Turner, Adam Clayton Powell, Jr., and Martin Luther King, Jr. This Black folk religion has never ceased providing the resources for radical movements in the Black community while the organized church receded into white evangelical pietism. Movements of Black nationalism, from the Moorish Science Temple to the Shrine of the Black Madonna, have their roots in a tradition which maintained a tenuous but persistent connection with Voodooism and the spirituality of the religions of Africa. It continues to be represented in the sects and cults of the Black ghetto and has periodically been enlisted as the base of contemporary movements led by such men as Imamu Tmeer Baraka, Maulana Ron Karenga, and Brother Imari of the Republic of New Africa. It is reflected in the National Negro Evangelical Association. It breaks out in Black music, Black drama, and the writing of the new Black 'alienation' poets. The Black middle class has generally sought to evade these influences, but even they are too deeply rooted in the masses, of whom Langston Hughes wrote:

But then there are the low-down folks, the so-called common element, and they are the majority – may the Lord be praised! The people who have their nip of gin on Saturday nights and are not too important to themselves or the community, or too well fed, or too learned to watch the lazy world go round. They live on 7th Street in Washington, or State Street in Chicago and they do not particularly care whether they are like white folks or anybody else. Their joy runs, bang! into ecstasy. Their religion soars to a shout. Work maybe a little today, rest a little tomorrow. Play awhile. Sing awhile. O, let's dance! These common people are not afraid of spirituals, as for a long time their more intellectual brethren were, and jazz is their child. They furnish a wealth of colourful, distinctive material for any artist because they still hold their own individuality in the face of American standardization.

This spirit is still the soul of Black religion and Black culture. Black theology must begin to understand and interpret it before it turns to white theologians for the substance of its reflection. The ebb and flow of Black folk religion is a constituent factor in every important crisis and development in the Black community. When the community is relatively integrated with the white society it recedes from Black institutions to form a hard core of unassimilable Black nationalism in an obscure corner of the social system – biding its time. When the community is hard-pressed, when hopes fade and the glimmer of light at the end of the tunnel is blocked out by resurgent white racism, then the essential folk element in Black religion exhibits itself again and begins anew to infiltrate the institutions which had neglected it. That is the meaning of the religion of Black Power today and the renewal of a radical Black theology within the contemporary Black church.

The second source of Black theology is in the writings and addresses of the Black preachers and the public men of the past. As white theology has its Augustine, its John Calvin, Martin Luther, Ulrich Zwingli, and John Wesley, Black theology has its Nat Turner, its Richard Allen, Martin Delany, Edward Blyden, and W. E. Burghardt Du Bois. Not all Black thinkers were ministers, but all of them were greatly influenced by Black religion. One cannot understand the genius of Black spirituality or the work of charismatic leaders like Martin King, Malcolm X or James Forman, without understanding how their interpretations of the Black experience were conditioned by great Black men of the past. Forman and Malcolm X belong as much to this theological tradition as Powell or King. In an important and neglected article written in 1964 Carleton Lee indicated the significance of prophecy in the Black community as spiritual vision, as a way of 'forth-telling' the transcendent meaning of history revealed to the inspired imagination. To the extent that secular prophets draw upon the history of suffering and struggle in the Black community and point to its destiny as the fulfilment of the faith and hope of a stolen and oppressed people, they deal with insights, themes and motifs of the Black religious consciousness and interpret Black reality in ways that are either religious or are readily incorporated into a basically religious view of life.

As we have seen in the earlier chapters of this book the writings of the nineteenth-century Black philosophers and preachers lift up some of the seminal ideas of a Black Theology – liberation, self-help, elevation, chosenness, emigration and unity. These are some of the major themes, charged with religious significance, with which men like Payne, Crummell, Turner and Grimke were obsessed. The broad vistas of Black reality which these concepts encompass need to be prospected for the rich veins of theological insight they contain. Cone has made a beginning of this development of a theology rooted and grounded in the Black experience, but even in *A Black Theology of Liberation* he retains the traditional categories, and in so doing finds it necessary to use the arguments of white theologians to buttress his position. This is certainly not prohibited, but neither is it the only option available to Black theologians whose ancestors have not produced a systematic theology.

Black theology's interests lie in another direction. What is needed to think theologically about the corpus of Black opinion – both written and oral – is a 'new consciousness,' a new way of perceiving and ordering religious, cultural and political data from the Black community. This, of course, requires a new set of interpretative tools, a new hermeneutic. Henry H. Mitchell recognizes the need for the Black theologian to break the interpretative strictures of white theology when he observes:

Just as the new hermeneutic of Ebeling and others has sought to recapture the vital message of Luther and the Reformation Fathers for the benefit of their sons, so must the Black hermeneutic seek to look into the message of the Black past and see what the Black Fathers could be saying to Black people today.

Mitchell has not, however, developed that hermeneutic in his two propositions of communicating in the argot of the uneducated Black Baptist preacher, and 'Putting the gospel on a tell-it-like-it-is, nitty-gritty basis.' The problem is infinitely more difficult than that. It has to do with unpacking the mythology, folklore and norms of the Black community as reflected in its verbal tradition and literature, in order to discover the ways in which Black people have acted out and linguistically communicated their provisional and ultimate concerns under an exploitative system. What Franz Fanon has done for the native people of Algeria and the Antilles, must yet be done for the oppressed Blacks of the United States.

Although Fanon would not agree with its utility, such a Black hermeneutic will deal with the morphology of Black language, the meaning of Black music, poetry, the dance, and, as Mitchell himself has suggested, not only the content, but the accent and cadences of Black preaching. In other words, if the God of justice and liberation has identified himself with the struggle of Black humanity and has manifested himself, in special ways, in the Black sub-community of the United States, then theologians need to know much more about the life style of that community and look at it through the eyes of its formal and informal leaders of the past and present. Only so will they be able to unlock the secrets of understanding and communicating the gospel of freedom in a new and meaningful way.

Black people, as Du Bois continually reminded us, are 'a spiritual people.' The theology of the Black community is developed not in theological seminaries, but on the streets, in the taverns and pool halls, as well as in the churches. The evolution of the first African Societies into the African Methodist church or a group of Black youths from a fighting gang to a Black nationalist club, reforming ex-convicts and fighting dope pushers, will suggest more about the operative religion and ethics of the Black community than a study of the literature of the neighbourhood Sunday schools. It is out of this welter of knowledge of the thought, feeling and action of the Black fathers and the contemporary Black ghetto that a hermeneutic can be constructed which will make it possible for Black theologians to read back to the community an interpretation of its indigenous religion that will clarify its basic commitments and integrate Black values and institutions around the core of liberation.

The third source of Black theology are the traditional religions of Africa, the way those religions encountered and assimilated, or were assimilated by, Christianity, and the process by which African theologians are seeking to make the Christian faith indigenous and relevant to Africa today. Black people are not only a spiritual people – they are also an African people. The dispute about African survivals in Negro culture and religion will go on, but it is clear that Black people did not begin on the auction blocks of Charlestown and New Orleans, nor did their religious consciousness commence with the preaching of Christianity to the slaves. It is still possible to recover some of the major beliefs of the traditional religions of Nigeria, Dahomey, Ghana, and other parts of Africa from which our ancestors came. Their development and alteration may be traced to the islands of the Caribbean and, to a lesser extent, to the mainland. It may be true that the contributions of African religion have all but evaporated from Black Christianity in the United States, but we do not know enough about the psychic structure of Black people, about what the Jungian psychologists call 'the collective unconscious,' of Black Americans to be able to say with absolute assurance that nothing of African spirituality lies deeply impregnated in 'the souls of black folk.' In any event, Black people who have struggled for their humanity against the suffocating domination of a racist, Anglo-Saxon culture, need to examine in much greater detail the religious contributions of their ancient homeland, which arise out of a vastly different cultural matrix than Europe and America. Professor Charles Long of the University of Chicago has written:

> Our colleague Mircea Eliade said long ago that the West was in danger of provincialism through a lack of attention to the orientations and solutions of non-Western man. It would be difficult, if not impossible, to make the case for the non-Western identity of the black community in America, though several make this claim. The element of truth in this claim is that though we are Westerners, we are not Western in the same way as our compatriots, and thus we afford within America an entree to the *otherness* of America and the otherness of mankind.

Those contributions, among others, are: a deep sense of the pervasive reality of the spirit world, the blotting out of the line between the sacred and the profane, the practical use of religion in all of life; reverence for ancestors and their real or symbolic presence with us, the corporateness of social life, the source of evil in the consequences of an act rather than in the act itself, and the imaginative and creative use of rhythm – singing and dancing – in the celebration of life and the worship of God. All of these aspects of African religions were found in some form, however attenuated, in the Black religion of the eighteenth and nineteenth centuries and were absorbed into Black Christianity in the Caribbean, South America and the United States. The feeling, spontaneity and freedom in Black religion and life had much to do with their resistance to complete whitenization, but this is also related to the intrinsic discontinuity between African and European religiosity. Black theology must be concerned about the recovery of those values, particularly the recovery of the achievement of freedom, the freedom to be *Muntu* – a man or a woman – in the most profound meaning of that profound Bantu word.

The theological programme of African scholars for the Africanization of Christianity in modern Africa has much to say to Black theology's 'ghettoization' of the Christian faith in the United States. In either case, the purpose is not to impose the sterile thought-forms and traditions of Western Christianity upon the Black community, but by a new approach to general revelation to discover a new and creative *Theologia Africana* which can unveil the reality of the Eternal Christ in the life and destiny of his Black people. Related to this quest are the urgent political issues of liberation in southern Africa and the United States, social justice and development, the relationship of Christianity to the separatist and independent churches on both sides of the Atlantic, and the contribution of Africa and Black America to the great social revolution of the Third World. Only by a sympathetic and intensive dialogue between the new younger theologians of Africa and Black theologians in the United States and the Caribbean will it be possible to uncover the harmonies and disharmonies in Black religion and forge the theological and ideological links which can bind modern Africa and Black America together for the unimaginable possibilities of the future.

What of that future? Perhaps the most that can be said is that the reformation and revivification of the faith that has come down to us from Jesus of Nazareth awaits the unhindered contribution of the nonwhite peoples of the world and that Black people of Africa and America will play a crucial role in that development. It will be preceded by the end of divisive sectarianism and the beginning of ecumenism in the institution of Black religion in the United States, by increasing communication and emigration between African and Black American churchmen, and by the development of an incisively relevant theology – on both continents – which will free itself from the false consciousness and impiety of white Christianity and bind Black people together, inside and outside of churches, in the solidarity of a new faith in God and humanity.

It can only be a matter of judgment, based upon the history of the Black race, and faith in the grace of a God who does not reward us according to our iniquities, to affirm that the Black world will not repeat the inhumanities of the white world. And if this judgment and faith are vindicated, mankind will be the beneficiary and the reconciliation for which the whole Church of Christ prays will become a realized eschatological event.

Until that time, too remote to deflect Black people from the revolutionary tasks which lie at hand today, white men must take, with utmost seriousness, the words of the National Committee of Black Churchmen in its 'Message to the Churches from Oakland' in 1969 – the year of the Black Manifesto:

We black people are a religious people. From the earliest time we have acknowledged a Supreme Being. With the fullness of our physical bodies and emotions we have unabashedly worshipped Him with shouts of joy and tears of pain and anguish. We neither believe that God is dead, white, nor captive to some rationalistic and dogmatic formulation of the Christian faith which relates Him exclusively to the canons of the Old and New Testaments, and accommodate Him to the reigning spirits of a socio-technical age. Rather, we affirm that God is Liberator in the man Jesus Christ, that His message is Freedom, and that today He calls all men to be what they are in themselves, and among their own people, in the context of a pluralistic world society of dignity and self-determination for all. We believe that in a special way God's favour rests today upon the poor and oppressed peoples of the world and that He calls them to be the ministering angels of His judgment and grace, as His Kingdom of freedom and peace breaks in from the future upon a world shackled to ancient sins and virtues.

Ananias Mpunzi · *Black Theology as Liberation Theology*

Ananias Mpunzi, 'Black Theology as Liberation Theology', *Black Theology: the South African Voice* ed. Basil Moore, C. Hurst, London and John Knox, Atlanta 1973, pp.134-40

While the structural aspect of freedom is not to be ignored as unimportant, it also must not be regarded as freedom itself. There is also a sense in which freedom is an attitude of mind which can exist in any situation or in any structure. Not only can it exist in any structure, it must exist in any structure if there is to be any change in the structures that enslave.

This attitudinal aspect is beautifully expressed by Solzhenitzyn in *The First Circle*. Nerzhin, indefinitely detained in prison, refuses to see the slops served to the prisoners as slops. They are a sacrament. Perhaps the deep significance of this is that slops are for pigs. Prisoners are served slops because they are seen as pigs and are being encouraged to see themselves as pigs. But the sacrament is for humans. To see the prison slops as a sacrament is thus a tremendous act of self-affirmation – despite the prison and despite the slops. It is the attitude of mind that says: 'Think what you will of me. I know myself to be a person. And I will not allow your attitude towards me or your actions against me to crush me. I will be what I am despite you – a person utterly intent on affirming my humanity.'

This is a crucial aspect for blacks in South Africa. We have been treated as less than human. We have been debarred from having a say in making the decisions that intimately affect our lives. Whites have come to see us as dogs (signs reading 'No dogs or Bantu' are not uncommon). Our blackness has been seen as the sign of our non-humanness. It stands for that which is dark and evil. Our past is seen as a past of barbarism. We are seen as little more than a troop of baboons with remarkably human-like features! ...

For our sakes, therefore, we have the task both of affirming the humanity of others and helping them to affirm it for themselves when it seems as if they have denied it. Thus freedom also entails enabling black people, all black people everywhere, to affirm what they are – *black people* – and enabling white people to affirm what they are – just *ordinary* people, even though they are white.

We have seen that by freedom is meant those structures which support and strengthen us in our uniqueness as individuals and in our desire for community – and that attitude of mind in which we affirm our humanity as individuals and the humanity of others who constitute the community.

Black Theology is a situational theology. It asks theological questions which are vital to particular people in a particular situation – that is, to us, the black people in South Africa – and the questions are the questions *we* are asking. Thus the 'theological dimension' is that which refers to *us* in our black situation.

First, then, does Black Theology support us in our drive to be ourselves in our uniqueness? Does it lend its support to our need to affirm ourselves as persons, as black persons? Thus is Black Theology a theology of liberation in this personal sense? To answer this we point to the doctrine of Creation. Whatever is meant by this doctrine it cannot be the *deus ex machina*; the God who set the mechanism ticking and now leaves it to run on its own. If that is what is meant, then God is not *my* Creator. He may be the Creator of my distant forbears, but not *my* Creator. No one could possibly be interested in a God at that distance, so mind-bogglingly removed from us in our here and now. The 'beginnings' referred to in the doctrine of Creation are surely no explanation of the present. They are not an explanation at all. It is the declaration of a relationship. It declares the immediacy of God's relationship with *me*. It affirms that God loves me as a unique individual as a father loves his children as unique individuals and that God has a unique will for me, not a general will for all into which I must fit, just as a father has specific hopes and dreams for each of his children as individuals, not a general desire for them all as a block.

Thus any affirmation of God must also be an affirmation of the uniqueness of every individual. If this affirmation of God is not simply to be pious and irrelevant talk, then it must also entail that I have the room in which to give visible expression to my uniqueness.

If this is what the doctrine of Creation entails, then it entails also the Divine affirmation of my uniqueness. And if a relationship of love is entailed between God and the unique individual, and if love is the give-and-take of a mutual honouring and self-honouring, then I have no right whatever to deny my unique personality in any way. It is an insult to God the Creator if ever anyone does deny it and a greater insult if we ever allow this behaviour by others to lead us on to think of ourselves as less than precious and unique individuals.

Thus, as Christans, we must affirm again and again that we are people. But people come in all sorts of different colours, shapes and sizes. My humanity includes my thinness, my fatness, my shortness, my tallness, my big nose, my small ears, my blackness or my whiteness. I am not a person *despite* my big nose. I am a person because the big nose, the small ears, the thin frame and the blackness are mine. Without the totality that is me I am not me! Therefore, in affirming my humanity I must affirm everything that is me. I must affirm my blackness. God must also affirm it, otherwise he could not know me or have any dealings with me, and my blackness would exclude me from him. It would exclude me from being a person. This does not mean that we must simply affirm everything about ourselves in a way that leaves no room for change. We must claim and affirm those things which we cannot change (such as our blackness) and we must acknowledge those things we can change (such as our attitudes to our blackness). Among the things we can change there will be those we must affirm as good without any apology. But there will be attitudes and values which we ourselves cannot accept as good. We need to acknowledge and understand these and to work at becoming new.

Thus Black Theology claims that God affirms my uniqueness, and so my blackness. It goes further and says: 'Black person, you are a unique person, and you must express your uniqueness or die, and you must affirm your humanity or become the thing, the object, that others have deluded you into believing yourself to be'. On the one hand you must tear down every man-made barrier that restricts your freedom to be yourself, and to live God's unique will for you in vibrantly fulfilling life. On the other hand, you must affirm yourself as a human being no matter what your situation or what others may say or do to you. You dare not believe the lies that others would make you believe by the nature of their non-human relationship with you. You dare only believe the truth that God would have you believe by the nature of his self-affirming relationship with you. You must love the sign of your humanity which others treat as the sign of your lack of humanity. You must love your own black body – your blackness!

Black Theology has no room for the traditional Christian pessimistic view of man, the view that we are by nature overwhelmingly and sinfully selfish. We know only too well that our white Western acquisitive society tries to harness that good and beautiful and God-given thing, our self-awareness, self-esteem and longing to be ourselves in our uniqueness. It has tried to take this away from us and replace it by crass individualism. Then the white, Western Church has come in alongside this. It has said little and done less to change this pattern of subversion of our self-pride. But it has ranted against those who have fallen prey to its own devouring influence, and called upon us to deny and denounce ourselves as people. 'We are selfish, We are worms.' And we have believed this and then let others trample over us. This pessimism about man is therefore an ally in our own undermining of ourselves.

Black Theology will have no truck with this. It is true that we are often deluded and duped, but our need to be ourselves in our uniqueness and thus our blackness is not evidence of the rampaging evil inherent in us. It is the stirring of God calling us to be ourselves so that we might respond not as worms but as people, both to God and to others. We must respond as what we know ourselves to be : black people.

Black Theology is a powerful call to freedom for black people, calling us to throw off the psychological shackles and structural bonds that hold us in self-denying conformity and bondage to others.

But there is also the relational dimension to freedom. Does Black Theology call us also to freedom in this inter-personal dimension both in its structural form and in its attitudinal aspect?

At the heart of the Christian doctrine of God is the Trinity. Western theology has gone into metaphysical somersaults over this doctrine, but it is not a metaphysical doctrine. It is deeply and passionately human. Would that we could drop the ossified Greco-Roman credal confessions of the Trinity and give new human life to the doctrine. The doctrine again is not an hypothesis to explain anything. It is a vision of tomorrow, of people as they ought to be, not an explanation of yesterday. Talk about the Trinity is not talk about a God 'out there', but it is talk about the ultimate in human relationships. It is thus a visionary call to the new.

On the one hand the doctrine affirms the uniqueness of the 'persons' of the Trinity. They are themselves and no others. They are who they are. But at the same time – and this is vital – they are one. God is not any one of the unique three alone. God is the oneness of the community. And that community demands an equality of the unique persons and their inter-relationship. Their uniqueness grows out of and is expressed in their unity. And that unity is God. It is in the image of this God that man is made, hence our humanity is not the sum and total of our uniqueness. It is not enough to say that we are persons in our uniqueness, however vital it is to say that. We are persons in the unity that holds people in the powerful give-and-take of love and acceptance.

Black Theology asserts that people, made in the image of the Trinity among whose three 'persons' there is no superiority, are not meant to set up in authority over others to rule their lives. It says that man, with his longing for fellowship, will tear down every structure that sets about trying to rule over others; authoritarianism must be destroyed in every one of its manifestations, particularly its racialist manifestation.

The freedom of which Black Theology speaks thus demands an attitude of enormous respect for others, and that because of this attitude we will refuse to allow any man to humiliate himself because others choose to humiliate him. We must shout loud and clear and far and wide to anyone who will hear: 'You are persons made for love. Don't cut yourself off from that love by thinking and acting as if you were superior to anyone else, and especially by acting as if you were inferior to anyone else.' It demands also, however, that we bully no one; people are too precious. We dare not in this way destroy them and thus their uniqueness. But we will do everything else to make people stand up and be themselves in the community of self- and mutually-respecting people.

Thus Black Theology is a theology of liberation. Although it directs its voice to black people, it nonetheless hopes that white people also will hear and be saved. In its call to black people it says: 'You, black person, are unique. Your longing to express your uniqueness is the stirring call of God within you. So don't let anybody try to fence in your unique being. Throw off anything that would attempt to do so.' It also says 'You, black people, want and need a community of accepting love. This too is the call of God in your brother. Answer it, but do not bow down to your brother or you will make him not your brother but your king.' Thus it says: 'Share your living but do not sell yourselves. Love your brother and affirm him, but do not make him more than you.' And finally it says: 'Black person, you could not be you and not black. So affirm and love and glory in your blackness.'

When all of this is a reality within us we will be on the move again, and being on the move is the only state of freedom, for God is on the move. Freedom is not having arrived, it is not being God. It is rather struggling to arrive, it is struggling to understand and to respond to God – the God who is not yesterday's explanation but the vision of, and call to, tomorrow, and tomorrow, and tomorrow.

7 · Violence

Political theology must constantly face up to the question of violence. Any dialogue with Marxism comes up against this problem at some point. When faith hopes for this world then the future is in dispute, and confrontation with those who control the future is inevitable. The theology of revolution had to face the problem in stark form, but the theology of development encountered forms of violence more frightening if also more respectable. Liberation is constantly threatened by those who will not allow others to go free. And certainly black theology, stemming from a new cultural milieu which developed in association with black power and the Panthers, cannot and does not seek to avoid the question of violence.

This is not the place to attempt an exhaustive treatment of violence. We shall be concerned with the more limited question of how it is that violence has become an issue at all for Christians and therefore for theology. Violence is 'excessive, unrestrained or unjustifiable force'. There could be no violence without power or force. But while power and force are neutral things, to be used for good or evil, violence can never be neutral: by definition it is an evil thing. How has it come that violence is widely accepted as inevitable today, by Christians and non-Christians alike?

Not that Western culture has been innocent of all violence in the past. To the contrary, violence seems to have been endemic and the miracle is that in this century some of the most overt and brutal/brutalizing examples of violence have become socially unacceptable. It is rather that when such brutality was carried out by those in positions of authority it was not regarded as violence. Possibly deriving from the Pauline view of the individual's relationship to the state and those who rule, theology has tended to justify the magistrate as bearing the sword by the decree of God. It was more than a semantic point to say that authorized force is always justified, while unauthorized force is always violence. Violence could hardly be an issue for Christians by such a definition.

Today, however, there is a greater recognition of the possibility of unjustifiable force exercised by those in authority. The classical position has broken down. Those who rule may on occasion initiate injustice rather than restrain it. Those who govern may come to power by violent or at least devious means, and institute policies which serve their interests and the interests of their immediate supporters. These things are not new; there is a greater readiness today to condemn violence no matter what the position or standing of those responsible for it.

Further, today there is a greater awareness of the scale of violence. The father of a starving family could be hung for stealing a lamb: his accuser might be responsible for their condition and hundreds like them. A man with a mask over his face may hold up a passer-by: meanwhile a faceless industrialist may hold a whole community to ransom. A newspaper man may punish his son for telling a lie: he may work for a newspaper which wilfully distorts the truth.

For these and other reasons, violence is a much more ambiguous phenomenon today. The violence of the revolutionary is condemned by those who hold office, but the revolutionary speaks of the violence of oppressive and unjust policies. Those who protest against injustice may do violence to the majority, while the call for law and order can be a frightening invitation to violent repression.

But apart from the more subtle identification of violence today there is also the disturbing cult of violence. In time of war ordinary people do violent things, with reluctance and sometimes with disgust, but in this century we see different strands forming a cult of violence which is far from displaying nausea at such actions. There was the violence of the Right as exemplified by the Nazis in the 1930s and during World War II. But more recently there is the violence of the Left, associated once again with the views of Frantz Fanon. In *The Wretched of the Earth* we read that, 'At the level of individuals, violence is a cleansing force. It frees the native from his inferiority complex and from his despair and inaction; it makes him fearless and restores his self-respect.' Notice here that Fanon the psychiatrist is speaking of the therapeutic value of violence. There is no hesitation over advocating violence, no excusing of the necessity of violence. Rather, the poison of the serpent is prescribed as the cure for the disease. It should, of course, be pointed out that in contrast to the Nazis,

Fanon is speaking about an initial violent act exercised by those who previously had no power. He does not advocate violence as a basis for society in the long term. Even so his words have contributed to a fascination with violence among those who do not live as marginals and less-than-men.

Until recently violence was regarded as a moral question – or rather in view of the classical Erastian position of the main churches it was regarded as no question at all. Today it is an issue in the dispute about how the world is and how it should be. It derives from ethical or theological judgment about the present and a prophetic judgment about the future.

For this reason Rubem Alves is able to analyse violence in the context of hope. In *A Theology of Human Hope* he says that 'the fear of the future gives birth to violence.' Those who so possess the present as to fear change use their power to make sure that no tomorrow comes to threaten today. To them violence is whatever disturbs or threatens the world as it is. For the man who does not possess the world today, but rather suffers under it and longs for change, violence is quite different. 'It is whatever denies him a future, whatever aborts his project to create a new tomorrow; it is the power that keeps him prisoner of the futureless structures of a futureless world.'

There is the overt violence which enslaves and keeps men enslaved by brute force. There is economic violence which thrusts upon them a certain life and denies them an alternative. And there is cultural violence which closes the mind to aspirations towards human fulfilment. Far from being overtly violent this last form may take an enlightened approach, bringing many benefits and gifts – except a man's own future.

At the particular level the problem of violence today concerns the dilemma, not what I should do if subjected to violence, but what should I do if my neighbour is subjected to violence. At the more general level the problem concerns the appropriate attitude to those who refuse to allow a new future to emerge, who forcibly close doors and subtly close minds. When those who had power were regarded as licensed by God then violence could never be in the service of God. In this new situation in which violence is identified no matter the source, then the question is raised as to whether – in the last resort – violence might be used in order to restrain evil and prevent massive and widespread suffering. But beyond the issue of choosing the lesser evil, there is the question whether counter-violence can actually bring about good, whether it could bring liberation to the captives.

Helder Camara · *Violence – the Only Way?*

Helder Camara, *Church and Colonialism: The Betrayal of the Third World*, pp.101-102, 104-107, 108-111. © Sheed & Ward Ltd 1969. First American edition 1969 by Dimension Books, Inc. Used by permission of the publishers

The subject is certainly topical. It is true that violence belongs to all ages, but today it is perhaps more topical than ever; it is omnipresent, in every conceivable form: brutal, overt, subtle, insidious, underhand, blind, rational, scientific, solidly entrenched, anonymous, abstract, irresponsible.

It isn't difficult to speak of violence if it is either to condemn it out of hand, from afar, without bothering to examine its various aspects or seek its brutal, and regrettable, causes; or if it is to fan the flames from a safe distance, in the manner of an 'armchair Che Guevara'.

What is difficult is to speak of violence from the thick of the battle, when one realises that often some of the most generous and the most able of one's friends are tempted by violence, or have already succumbed to it. I ask you to hear me as one who lives in a continent whose climate is pre-revolutionary, but who, while he has no right to betray the Latin American masses, has not the right either to sin against the light or against love.

Here is a first basic remark, necessary to the understanding of the problematic of violence: the whole world is in need of a structural revolution. With regard to the underdeveloped countries, this fact is self-evident. From whatever standpoint one approaches the question – economic, scientific, political, social, religious – it soon becomes obvious that a summary, superficial reform is absolutely insufficient. What is needed is a reform in depth, a profound and rapid change; what we must achieve – let's not be afraid of the word – is a structural revolution.

As Paul vi has recently said:

> One thing is certain, the present situation must be faced courageously, and the injustice it comprises must be fought and overcome. Audacious transformations and a profound renewal are the price of development. Reforms must be urgently undertaken, without delay. Everyone must generously play his part.

Economically speaking, it is common knowledge that the underdeveloped countries suffer from internal colonialism. A small group of rich and powerful people in each country maintains its power and wealth at the expense of the misery of millions of the population. This regime is still semi-feudal, with a semblance of a 'patriarchal' system, but in reality a total absence of personal rights; the situation is sub-human, the conditions those of slavery. The rural workers, who are nothing more than pariahs, are denied access to the greater part of the land, which lies idle in the hands of rich landowners who are waiting for its value to rise ...

If we Latin-American christians assume our responsibility in face of the underdevelopment of the continent we can and must work to promote radical changes in all sectors of social life, particularly in politics and education. Politics must not remain the preserve of a privileged few, who stand in the way of basic reforms by betraying them or agreeing to them on paper only. Education is so far below the needs of technology – itself in constant evolution – that the unrest of our students is easy to understand. They have no time for the superficial, timid, and empty university reforms that are imposed upon them.

My remarks about Latin America can, more or less, be transposed to the whole of the underdeveloped world, which is in crying need of a structural revolution.

It is harder to understand that the developed countries are also in need of a structural revolution. Isn't their advanced state of development a proof that they have achieved success? Why should they need a revolution? Let us glance for a moment at the two most successful forms of development, under the capitalist and socialist regimes, as exemplified by the United States and the Soviet Union.

The United States is a living demonstration of the internal contradiction of the capitalist system : it has succeeded in creating underdeveloped strata within the richest country in the world – 30 million Americans live in a situation below the dignity of the human condition : it has succeeded in provoking a fratricidal war between whites and blacks; under the guise of anti-communism, but in fact driven by a lust for prestige and the expansion of its sphere of influence, it is waging the most shameful war the world has ever known. The dominant system in the United States is so irrational in its rationalisation, as they call it, that it has succeeded in creating a one-dimensional, 'robot' existence, to such an extent that young Americans of different cultural traditions feel called to build a more just and more human society by transforming the social context and humanising technology.

The Soviet Union considers itself motivated solely by scientific humanism, since it takes its inspiration from marxism. In practice, however, under the pretext of defending itself from the contamination of capitalism it perpetuates the iron curtain and the wall of shame; it refuses all pluralism within the socialist camp – the Soviet Union and red China face each other like two capitalist powers; and it considers marxism to be an untouchable dogma.

Marx failed to distinguish between the essence of christianity and the weakness of christians who, in practice, often reduced it to an opium for the people. But today there is a change of attitude among christians. Now, even in practice, there is an effort to preach and live a christianity that is by no means an alienated or alienating force, but that is incarnated among men, following the example of Christ. This change has not yet been understood by the Soviet Union.

The Soviet Union and the United States have just furnished yet one more example of their bad faith and incomprehension of the Third World, at New Delhi.

It is in vain that Asia at Bangkok, Africa at Algiers, and Latin America at Tequendama, in vain that the Third World in its letter from Algiers continues to repeat that the problems which vitiate relations between rich and poor countries are not a question of aid, but of *justice* on a world scale.

The two 'super-powers', supreme examples of capitalism and socialism, remain blind and deaf, enclosed and imprisoned in their egoism. How can the developed world be prevented from leaving the underdeveloped world each day further and further behind. Today, 85%, tomorrow 90%, rot in misery in order to make possible the excessive comfort of 15%, tomorrow 10%, of the world's population. Who can now fail to understand the need for a structural revolution in the developed world?

Before asking whether the structural revolution needed by the world necessarily supposes violence, it must be underlined that violence already exists and that it is wielded, sometimes unconsciously, by the very people who denounce it as a scourge of society.

It exists in the underdeveloped countries: the masses in a subhuman situation are exploited violently by privileged and powerful groups. It is well known that if the masses attempt to unite by means of education at grass roots level based on the popular culture, if they form trade unions or cooperatives, their leaders are accused of treason or communism. This has aptly been described as follows: 'they rebel against the established disorder, so they are classed as outlaws ... They must disappear so that order may reign.' An orderly disorder!

As for 'law', it is all too often an instrument of violence against the weak, or else it is relegated to the fine phrases of documents and declarations, such as the Declaration of the Rights of Man, whose second decade the world is commemorating this year. A good way of celebrating this anniversary would be for the United Nations Organisation to verify if one or two of these rights are in fact respected in two-thirds of the world.

Violence also exists in the developed world, whether capitalist or socialist. In this respect, there are certain disquieting signs which speak for themselves. Negroes pass from non-violence to violence. The black apostle of non-violence is felled to the consternation and shame of all men of goodwill ... Faced with the new Czechoslovakia, the Soviet Union's uneasiness is evident and, under the pretext of safeguarding the unity of the socialist camp, it rekindles the ideological battle against the capitalist world ...

Even more scandalous is the violence perpetrated by the developed world against the underdeveloped countries, as we have already seen in connection with the failure of the Second UNCTAD Conference at New Delhi.

Faced with this triple violence – that which exists in the Third World, or in the developed world, or that done to the former by the latter – it isn't hard to understand the possibility of thinking, speaking and acting in terms of a liberating violence, of a redemptive violence.

If the élites of the Third World haven't the courage to rid themselves of their privileges and to bring justice to the millions living in sub-human conditions; if the governments concerned content themselves with reforms on paper, how can one restrain the youth who are tempted by radical solutions and violence? In the developed countries on both sides, how long will it be possible to restrain the ardour of youth, the spearhead of tomorrow's unrest, if the signs of disquiet and violence continue to multiply? How long will nuclear bombs be more powerful than the poverty bomb which is forming in the Third World?

Allow me the humble courage to take up a position on this issue. I respect those who feel obliged in conscience to opt for violence – not the all too easy violence of armchair guerilleros – but those who have proved their sincerity by the sacrifice of their life. In my opinion, the memory of Camilo Torres and of Che Guevara merits as much respect as that of Martin Luther King. I accuse the real authors of violence: all those who, whether on the right or the left, weaken justice and prevent peace. My personal vocation is that of a pilgrim of peace, following the example of Paul VI;

personally, I would prefer a thousand times to be killed than to kill.

This personal position is based on the gospel. A whole life spent trying to understand and live the gospel has produced in me the profound conviction that if the gospel can, and should, be called revolutionary it is in the sense that it demands the conversion of each of us. We haven't the right to enclose ourselves within our egoism; we must open ourselves to the love of God and the love of men. But is it enough to turn to the beatitudes – the quintessence of the gospel message – to discover that the choice for christians seems clear: we christians are on the side of non-violence, which is by no means a choice of weakness or passivity. Non-violence means believing more passionately in the force of truth, justice and love than in the force of wars, murder and hatred.

If this appears to be mere moralising, be patient a moment. If the option for non-violence has its roots in the gospel, it is also based on reality. You ask me to be realistic? Here is my answer: If an explosion of violence should occur anywhere in the world, and especially in Latin America, you may be sure that the great powers would be immediately on the spot – even without a declaration of war – the super-powers would arrive and we would have another Vietnam. You ask for more realism? Precisely because we have to achieve a structural revolution it is essential to plan in advance a 'cultural revolution' – but in a new sense. For if mentalities do not undergo a radical change then structural reforms, from the base, will remain at the theoretical stage, ineffective.

I should like now to address a few remarks especially to the young. To the youth of the underdeveloped countries I put this question: what is the point of acceding to power if you lack models adapted to your situation, to your countries? Up till now you have been offered solutions which are viable only for developed countries. While we christians try to exert a moral pressure, even more courageously, on those who are responsible for the situation in our countries, you should try to prepare yourselves for the responsibilities that await you tomorrow; try above all to help the masses to become a people. You know only too well that material and physical underdevelopment leads to intellectual, moral and spiritual underdevelopment.

To the youth of developed countries, both capitalist and socialist, I would say: Instead of planning to go to the Third World to try and arouse violence there, stay at home in order to help your rich countries to discover that they too are in need of a cultural revolution which will produce a new hierarchy of values, a new world vision, a global strategy of development, the revolution of mankind.

Allow me to make one final remark. I have just come from Berlin, where I was invited to the World Congress of International Catholic Youth Movements. In that divided city I wondered how Europe could accept the dismembering of Berlin – symbol of so many divisions in the whole world. Why does mankind allow itself to be divided and torn asunder, from east to west, and even more profoundly from north to south?

It is only those who achieve an inner unity within themselves and possess a worldwide vision and universal spirit who will be fit instruments to perform the miracle of combining the violence of the prophets, the truth of Christ, the revolutionary spirit of the gospel – but without destroying love.

Camilo Torres · *Message to Christians*

From *Revolutionary Priest: The Complete Writings and Messages of Camilo Torres*, ed. John Gerassi, Jonathan Cape, London and Random House, Inc., NY 1971. © 1971 by Random House, Inc. Used by permission of John Gerassi, Jonathan Cape and Random House, Inc.

Laicization

When circumstances prevent men from actively consecrating their lives to Christ, it is the priest's duty to combat these circumstances even if he must forfeit the right to officiate at Eucharistic rites, which have meaning only if Christians are so consecrated.

Within the present structure of the church, it has become impossible for me to continue acting as priest in the external aspects of our religion. However, the Christian priesthood consists not only of officiating at external ritual observances. The Mass, which is at the centre of the priesthood, is fundamentally communal. But the Christian community cannot worship in an authentic way unless it has first effectively put into practice the precept of love for fellow man. I chose Christianity because I believed that in it I would find the purest way to serve my fellow man. I was chosen by Christ to be a priest forever because of the desire to consecrate my full time to the love of my fellow man.

As a sociologist, I have wanted this love to be translated into efficient service through technology and science. My analysis of

Colombian society made me realize that revolution is necessary to feed the hungry, give drink to the thirsty, clothe the naked, and procure a life of well-being for the needy majority of our people. I believe that the revolutionary struggle is appropriate for the Christian and the priest. Only by revolution, by changing the concrete conditions of our country, can we enable men to practise love for each other.

Throughout my ministry as priest, I have tried in every way possible to persuade the laymen, Catholic or not, to join the revolutionary struggle. In the absence of a massive response, I have resolved to join the revolution myself, thus carrying out part of my work of teaching men to love God by loving each other. I consider this action essential as a Christian, as a priest, and as a Colombian. But such action, at this time, is contrary to the discipline of the present church. I do not want to break the discipline of the church, but I also do not want to betray my conscience.

Therefore, I have asked his Eminence the Cardinal to free me from my obligations as a member of the clergy so that I may serve the people on the temporal level. I forfeit one of the privileges I deeply love – the right to officiate as priest at the external rites of the church. But I do so to create the conditions that will make these rites more authentic.

I believe that my commitment to live a useful life, efficiently fulfilling the precept of love for my fellow man, demands this sacrifice of me. The highest standard by which human decisions must be measured is the all-surpassing love that is true charity. I accept all the risks that this standard demands of me.

Message to Christians

The convulsions caused by the political, religious, and social events of recent times may have sown a great deal of confusion among Colombian Christians. At this decisive moment in our history, we Christians must take a firm stand on the essential bases of our religion.

In Catholicism the main thing is love for one's fellow man: '... he who loves his fellow man has fulfilled the Law' (Romans xiii, 8). For this love to be genuine, it must seek to be effective. If beneficence, alms, the few tuition-free schools, the few housing projects – in general, what is known as 'charity' – do not succeed in feeding the hungry majority, clothing the naked, or teaching the unschooled masses, we must seek effective means to achieve the well-being of these majorities. These means will not be sought by the privileged minorities who hold power, because such effective means generally force the minorities to sacrifice their privileges. For example, employment could be increased by investing the capital now leaving Colombia in dollars in the creation of new job opportunities here in the country. But, due to the virtually daily devaluation of the Colombian peso, those with money and power are never going to prohibit currency exportation, because it frees them from devaluation.

Thus, power must be taken from the privileged minorities and given to the poor majorities. If this is done rapidly, it constitutes the essential characteristic of a revolution. The revolution can be a peaceful one if the minorities refrain from violent resistance. Revolution is, therefore, the way to obtain a government that will feed the hungry, clothe the naked, and teach the unschooled. Revolution will produce a government that carries out works of charity, of love for one's fellows – not for only a few but for the majority of our fellow men. This is why the revolution is not only permissible but obligatory for those Christians who see it as the only effective and far-reaching way to make the love of all people a reality. It is true that 'there exists no authority except from God' (Romans xiii, 1). But St Thomas teaches that it is the people who concretely have the right to authority.

When the existing authority is against the people, it is not legitimate, and we call it a tyranny. We Christians can and must fight against tyranny. The present government is tyrannical because it receives the support of only 20 per cent of the voters and because its decisions emanate from the privileged minorities.

The temporal defects of the church must not shock us. The church is human. The important thing is to believe that it is also divine and that if we Christians fulfil our obligation to love our fellow man, we are thereby strengthening the church.

I have given up the duties and privileges of the clergy, but I have not ceased to be a priest. I believe that I have given myself to the revolution out of love for my fellow man. I have ceased to say Mass to practise love for my fellow man in the temporal, economic, and social spheres. When my fellow man has nothing against me, when he has carried out the revolution, then I will return to offering Mass, God permitting. I think that in this way I follow Christ's injunction: 'Therefore, if thou art offering thy gift at the altar, and there rememberest that thy brother has any-thing against thee, leave thy gift before the altar and go first to be reconciled to thy brother, and then come and offer thy gift' (Matthew v, 23-4). After the revolution we Colombians will be aware that we are establishing a system oriented towards the love of our neighbour. The struggle is long; let us begin now.

Jacques Ellul · *The Fight of Faith*

Jacques Ellul, *Violence*, SCM Press, London 1970 and Seabury Press, NY 1969, pp.168-75. © 1969 by The Seabury Press, Inc. Used by permission

This violence of love is an expression of spiritual violence. Spiritual violence, however, is neither acceptable nor possible except on three conditions. First, it must reject all human means of winning a victory or registering effects. I should like to broadcast the innumerable Old Testament passages which tell how God opposed his people's use of 'normal' means of settling conflicts – weapons, chariots, horsemen, alliances, diplomatic manoeuvres, revolution (Jehu) – and bade them put their trust in the Lord's word and his faithfulness. This is radical spiritual violence. And God lets us choose. Paul also lets us choose. He tells us that he did not come 'proclaiming the testimony of God in lofty words or wisdom,' lest rhetoric and philosophy hide the power of the Spirit. I do not say that we are forbidden to employ human means. I say that when we do employ them (and we are not condemned for doing so!) we take away from the Word that has been entrusted to us all its force, its efficacity, its violence. We turn the Word into a sage dissertation, an explication, a morality of moderation. When we use political or revolutionary means, when we declare that violence will change the social system we are *thus* fighting in defence of the disinherited, our violence demolishes the spiritual power of prayer and bars the intervention of the Holy Spirit. Why? Because this is the logic of the whole revelation of God's action – in Abraham the disinherited wanderer, in Moses the stutterer, in David the weakling, in Jesus the Poor Man. Provided we reject human means, our spiritual intervention may become effectual spiritual violence. Of course, this involves risk. But if we do not take the risk, we can only take the middle way, and even if we plunge into armed, violent, extremist revolution, we are still among the lukewarm. I need hardly say that this is no brief for the traditional sanctimonious patter of the churches that have retreated into their piety, or for the mediocre, musty, introverted, and highly moral lives of many Christians, who are impervious to the violence of love and the power of the Spirit. It is only at a certain level of intensity, urgency, spiritual earnestness that the problem of this choice arises. And, as I said, the choice one makes is decisive, for only if it is the right one is spiritual action possible and spiritual violence legitimate.

Hence a second condition, consequent to the first. Spiritual violence and the violence of love totally exclude physical or psychological violence. Here the violence is that of the intervention of the Spirit of God. The Spirit will not intervene, will not rush in with explosive power, unless man leaves room – that is, unless man himself intervenes. It is precisely because in this fight the Christian has to play a role that no one else can fill – it is precisely for this reason that the Christian can accept no other role. He makes himself ridiculous when he tries to be a politician, a revolutionary, a guerrilla, a policeman, a general. Spiritual violence radically excludes both the physical violence and the participation in violent action that go with such roles. It is not authentic spiritual violence unless it is only *spiritual* violence. It plays its role of violence with, before and against God (the struggle of Abraham and Jacob) only when it refrains from any other violence. And this exclusion is required not only by the decision of God as recorded in the Scriptures, but also and to a greater degree, by the fact that the Christian can never consider violence the *ultima ratio*. We have seen all along that this is the argument regularly trotted out to justify violence. Violence, we are told, is legitimate when the situation is such that there is absolutely no other way out of it. The Christian can never entertain this idea of 'last resort.' He understands that for the others it may be so, because they place all their hopes in this world and the meaning of this world. But for the Christian, violence can be at most a second-last resort. Therefore it can never be justified in a Christian life, because it would be justified only by being really a last resort. The Christian knows only one last resort, and that is prayer, resort to God.

Please, let no one bring up again the inevitable and useless argument: 'We must do what we pray for, we cannot ask for daily bread for ourselves without giving daily bread to others.' I accept that as expressing a pastoral point of view and a serious attitude towards prayer. But that is not at all what prayer means. To say 'Our Father' is to put oneself into God's hands, to submit to his decisions, to trust in his mercy – and to appeal the unjust judgments of men to the just judgment of God. No, the idea of violence as *ultima ratio* is intolerable, and for that reason (among other reasons) the Christian cannot take any part of it. It is precisely in the midst of violence that he must witness to another resort and another hope, just as serious, as efficacious, as dependable as activism. To be sure, if he does this where violence and revolution are rife, he will be laughed at or treated like a coward or an opium dealer. In our society, it is much more difficult to stand up for the truth than to go to Colombia and fight for justice or to join the Ku Klux Klan to quell the black uprising. But if the Christian does not bear witness to truth, he is just as hypocritical as his forefathers were when they used Christianity to justify commercial ventures or to support their social order. When some kind of sociopolitical activity is the important thing, faith in Christ is only a means. Nowadays, for a Christian to say that violence (any kind of violence, whatever its origin and its aim) is the *ultima ratio* is to signalize his infidelity – and the primary meaning of that word is 'absence of faith.'

So we come to the third condition in relation to spiritual violence. If it is true spiritual violence, it is based on earnest faith – faith in the possibility of a miracle, in the Lordship of Jesus Christ, in the coming of the Kingdom through God's action, not ours, faith in *all* of the promise (for the promise must not be taken apart into bits and pieces, in the manner of the theologians of revolution). This is a faith that concerns not only the salvation of the believer; it concerns the others, the unbelievers; it carries them and takes responsibility for them; it is convinced that for these others, too, there is a truth, a hope greater than revolutionary action, even if this hope does not attach to the material side of life. All of which is to say that there is a real choice to be made here (and making it will surely be the heaviest burden placed upon the Christian who tries to live his faith). We cannot, by taking neither, play on both sides. But if we witness to spiritual violence before the others, we cannot go on living in material violence, living for ourselves, protecting our own interests or our society. The choice is between violence and the Resurrection. Faith in the Resurrection – which is the supreme spiritual violence because it is victory over the necessity of death – excludes the use of every other violence. And it is true that, the Resurrection being accomplished, we can and must proclaim consolation and reconciliation. For men today have much greater *need* of true consolation than of economic growth, of reconciliation than of appeals to hate and violence.

I know that by saying that I am prompting the accusation:

'This kind of discourse is an attempt to divert the poor from revolution; this is the talk of a watchdog of capitalism and the bourgeois order.' I know. I have two things to say in answer. First, no one can hold 'this kind of discourse' unless (as we have seen) he is also and simultaneously acting as spokesman for the oppressed and attacking the unjust order with every nonviolent weapon. Second, even if such discourse were uttered by a liar using it to defend other interests (and I doubt that such a liar would use it), it would still be true. Nevertheless, we Christians must always bear this accusation in mind, lest we speak such words lightly. We should accept it as an alert (sounded by the perspicacious non-Christian) that bids us to be aware before God of what we can proclaim in truth to the poor in our midst. But we must also be thoroughly aware that when we, as Christians, hold a discourse on violence, it is our lack of faith that speaks.

The whole meaning of the violence of love is contained in Paul's word that evil is to be overcome with good (Romans 12: 17-21). This is a generalization of the Sermon on the Mount. And it is important for us to understand that this sermon shows what the violence of love is. Paul says, 'Do not let yourself be overcome by evil.' This then is a fight – and not only spiritual, for Paul and the whole Bible are very realistic and see that evil is constantly incarnated. But to be overcome by evil does not mean that he who is overcome is weaker, inferior, beaten, eliminated; no, it means that he is led to play evil's game – to respond by using evil's means, to do evil. That is what it means to be overcome by evil, to respond to violence by violence. Paul bids us *overcome* evil with good, and this, too, is the imagery of contest. We are not to bend or yield before evil, nor to act like cowards or impotent weaklings: we are to overcome, to *surmount* evil, to go beyond it, to stand on a terrain that evil cannot reach, use weapons that evil cannot turn back on us, seek a victory that evil can never attain!

Choosing different means, seeking another kind of victory, renouncing the marks of victory – this is the only possible way of breaking the chain of violence, of rupturing the circle of fear and hate. I would have all Christians take to heart this word of Gandhi's: 'Do not fear. He who fears, hates; he who hates, kills. Break your sword and throw it away, and fear will not touch you. I have been delivered from desire and from fear *so that I know* the power of God.' These words show that the way Christ appointed is open to all, that the victory of good over evil benefits not only Christians but non-Christians also. In other words, that if the

Christian knows that the fight of faith promises *this* victory, it is not only his victory but others' too. If he sees that the others are obsessed by violence and can find no other way, he has to play another card with them and for them. How is it that, in the midst of the racial struggle going on in the United States today, so many white Christians leave to black Christians the appanage of nonviolence? Why do they not take the way of repentance and conciliation in the face of black violence – repentance for the violences the whites committed in the past? Why, in the face of the black violence they provoked, do they not now seek peace *at any price*? It is only by love that is total, without defence, without reservation, love that does not calculate or bargain, that the white Christian will overcome the evil of revolution, arson, and looting. I make bold to say this even though I am not in the United States; I have lived through similar situations elsewhere.

Neither exaltation of power nor the search for vengeance will ever solve any human situation. In accepting death, Jesus Christ showed us the only possible way. We may refuse to take it. But we must realize that when we refuse we are left with one alternative – increasing the sum of evil in the world. And we ought to be honest and renounce all pretensions to the Christian faith. Surely we shall not use the suffering of the others whose side we take as an excuse for evading the only way that is open for faith. And if vengeance must be exacted, if a judgment, a condemnation must be pronounced, they are the Lord's alone. This holds on the social as well as on the individual level. To pretend to end exploitation by force is to eliminate the exploiter by violence, to exercise the judgment that is God's to exercise. For as we have seen throughout this investigation, there can be no use of violence without hate, without judgment, without abomination. Violence and revolution – let them continue! But without the presence and justification of Christians. This does not mean, however, that Christians are permitted to execrate or judge those who do take part in violence and revolution.

Will it be said then that the Christians are absent from the world? Curious that 'presence in the world' should mean accepting the world's ways, means, objectives; should mean helping hate and evil to proliferate! Christians will be sufficiently and completely present in the world if they suffer with those who suffer, if they seek out with those sufferers the one way of salvation, if they bear witness before God and man to the consequences of injustice and the proclamation of love.

8 · Christian Resistance

Political theology developed in Europe but has now moved to the Third World. In its early stages it was written against the background of a growing radical movement in European politics which finally burst upon the streets and campuses of the continent. Now political theology has spread abroad and the typewriters fall silent, but then the streets are silent too and there is a quite definite mood of dismay and disillusionment where previously there was excitement and optimism. The idealism of the young Marx is less in evidence today than a few years ago. The movement which hoped has lost its dynamism. The expectation of a new man and a new society has faded. In Europe 'realism' has fallen like a shroud upon the plans for an alternative world. Politics has been handed back to the politicians and the art of the possible has become once again the arrangement of the probable and the all too predictable.

In America the situation is much the same. The movement for a new tomorrow and alternative future for America was increasingly caught up in opposition to the war in Vietnam. This was inevitable but it had unfortunate side effects. Totalitarian regimes are sometimes accused of putting a country on a war footing in order to deflect attention from conditions within the country. The effect in America was substantially the same. The movement, which had begun as a protest about American life, became focused as a protest against Vietnam. In 1968 and again in 1972 the old party machines rolled on, as formidable as ever and even more dangerous to the amateurs who got in their way. The movement increasingly turned in on itself and asked only that it be allowed to live quietly without too much interference from mainstream America. The moment was exactly right for the administration to end the war, for the war was the only rallying point left for the movement. (The details made no difference: it was an official ending of an unofficial war – or rather it was a non-ending of an actual war. Either way the movement came to an end.)

Like players who in defeat become spectators of the next round, we in Europe and America look to the Third World to see if they can do better. It is all turning out as Fanon predicted. Was Europe not better placed to achieve the new man and the new society than those backward countries which had arguably still to enter the twentieth century? Now in their own way and in their own time some of them begin to build what we have hardly conceived of. We find ourselves hoping for them, and hoping for ourselves through them. The temptation is to go and join them. But it is a temptation and for most of us one to be resisted. Or if we go then let us remember the words of the late Bishop Manuel Larrain, president of the Conference of Latin American Bishops. In *Celebration of Awareness* Ivan Illich records the words, and though originally describing missionaries their application is much wider. 'They may be useless to us in Latin America, but they are the only North Americans whom we will have the opportunity to educate. We owe them that much.' And Archbishop Helder Camara has appealed to the youth of Europe to work at home for those changes which will allow the Third World to go its own way unimpeded.

What is left then, to those who live on in the West? Commitment, involvement, action led in the end to nothing. For those who look to a new tomorrow there is no longer a politics of hope, neither hope for politics. The New Left is as lacking in credibility as the members of the parliamentary club. Where else to begin but with ourselves? Throughout the development of political theology, the Christians have seemed to follow the lead of the politicos: the theory, the analysis, the goals and the actions have been already there. But Christians may well have reflected on one detail often dismissed as unimportant, namely the fact that those who speak about the new man and the new society seldom embody the life of which they speak. Those who call for a new tomorrow seldom anticipate that new day now. Christians may well reflect on a curious dialectic present in the New Testament. When Jesus speaks of the Kingdom it is something which is coming, yet something which is already breaking in upon men in the present. When Paul speaks of the future he can already point to an earnest or guarantee (surety/downpayment) already available. The credibility of the promise is that its fulfilment is already being experienced now.

The political movement in the West may have run out of strength and courage, vision and perseverance because it was always arranging for a new society but never embodying it. In this way the movement was not altogether distinguishable from the society it claimed to oppose. The members of the movement may have been fundamentally agreed with society in general that they were not going to bear the cost of the transition to the new, were not going to risk themselves for the sake of the future of all. Once again, Christians might well reflect that this attitude is alien to the witness of Jesus to the Kingdom, he who was willing to risk his all for the future of all.

The culmination of political theology might therefore be the discovery for Christians that their own faith is much more subversive of the present age than anything deriving from purely political analysis. It is surprising not so much that this is so, but that it could ever have been overlooked. The cross was a symbol of resistance before it was ever mythologized into an eternal altar. The new life of which Jesus spoke and in his own life concretely promised could hardly be in starker contrast to the life of the world at that time, or in this present time. We tend to think of liberation in terms of political freedom, yet was there ever a man so liberated as Jesus even as he walked a prisoner to his own death? Was there ever a community as liberated as the early church even when in chains they were drawn to the place of the beasts? Little people though they were, they were beyond the power of Rome. And for this reason terror was not in their hearts, but in the hearts of the rulers of this world. The Romans saw with unclouded vision that when the meek are beyond their control then the world begins to slip from the hands of the strong. Those of The Way in all innocence were turning the world upside down.

The cross was the symbol of resistance to the authority of the world (both political and religious) when authority demanded respect and obedience for the wisdom of this world. But lest we become over romantic, the cross was also the instrument of torture and murder by which the rulers of the world hoped to break the allegiance to the new or at least intimidate others from following that way. The witness of Jesus and the early church is that to follow this way is beyond our normal resources, and the believer must have recourse to the Bible, contemplation and the eucharist. If we were foolhardy enough to attempt this way then we should need such resources within the community. In *America is Hard to Find* Daniel Berrigan tells us that 'The time will shortly be upon us, if it is not already here, when the pursuit of contemplation becomes a strictly subversive activity.' To deepen and strengthen a new life which is not the life of this world is a subversive activity.

Our culture is based upon as many myths as any ancient culture and like theirs, our myths seem self-evident. There are myths about how we should lead our lives and what it takes to be happy; there are myths about how we should behave towards our neighbours and how we should be governed. There are myths about what can be changed and what must always remain just so. We have all been brought up within the spell of these myths, and are in constant danger of being overcome by them. If in the Bible, contemplation and the eucharist we find resources by which such spells are dispelled, such untruths belied, then we are enabled to continue in a path which undermines the life of our society and initiates the despoiling of the culture of the strong. Yet it is the culture of the strong and they will oppose any threat to their possession of the world. There is a cross to be borne in the throwing away of that which ties us to the way of the world, and the cross imposed by those who like some modern pharaoh will not see us go gladly. But there is the paradox that the early church experienced, that the keeping of The Way is no burden.

Daniel Berrigan · *Letter to the Young Jesuits*

Daniel Berrigan, *America is Hard to Find*, SPCK, London and Doubleday, NY 1973, pp.128-29, 131-32, 135-39. © 1972 by Daniel Berrigan

St Ignatius Day, 1971

Dear Brothers beyond the wall:

I am setting down a rather rambling newsletter to greet you on St Ignatius day. Also to thank you in the name of many brothers in prison for the stand you have taken against the draft.

Thanks are certainly in order. On reflection, nothing could be more fitting than that men of peace express their abomination of a free-fodder system that processes the living for death.

Let me, however, suggest a caveat. Your action is late. It was delayed undoubtedly by the deferment offered the churches by the state – an arrangement whose consequences is a deferred development of awareness. A tardy act on behalf of life is certainly better than none. At the same time, one is humbled by the reflection that others have gone further and faster to the heart of the matter (resistance) and have paid a far more grievous price than we clerics.

Further, an action of this type is self-defeating unless it opens you to the possibility of further resistance. It would I think be tragic if you declared your independence of empire, only to return home, confident that you had done your thing. Home to what? one asks. Institutions as usual, church as usual, Jesuits as usual? The poor of your cities neglected as usual, racism as usual, fail-safe war as usual? I suggest your draft statement has only started something you are honour-bound to pursue; either that, or you have started nothing at all, in which case your own sense of honour is surely in question.

Let me quite simply share my views in regard to resistance. Resistance to the war-ridden, blood-shot state is the form that human life is called to assume today. It is also the simplest, most logical way of translating the gospel into an argot that will be exact and imaginative at once. It is an occasion of rebirth, and a bloody one. It is also a choice. We will either die in our old skins (with all that implies of violated promise, personal despair) or we will come to second birth by giving our lives for others. (I plead guilty here to a fundamentalism that prison tends to hasten.) One gets reborn by saying 'No' to the state – a 'No' loud and clear enough to be heard, to trouble Leviathan.

We are required, Camus says somewhere, to be neither victim nor executioner. To be what, then? The alternative is the nub of the matter. Somewhere in the bowels of the state, or the bowels of the church, is the new birth gestating? One who will neither kill as required by good citizenship, nor be victimized by cowardice, silence, slavish obedience, cultural me-too-ism? Surely God and ourselves long for such a one to get born.

The new man or the new woman will certainly not be the product of spontaneous generation; born of our fevered and impure blood, an act of God – but just as certainly an act of ourselves. I assure you such men and women are coming to birth daily in prison. A helping word, a constant word of truth, an unselfish will to live for others – these bring us to birth.

I pray such a one is being born among you, too. No one else can respond to the staggering, life-and-death character of our needs today. You know these needs as well as I. You know too that the old comfortable arrangements between church and state are helpless to generate newness. To the contrary, they prolong the stereotyped, lethal 'solutions' of war, racism, poverty.

And in proportion as we envision a life based on such arrangements, or benefit because of them, I think we dishonour Christ. More, we join in principle the destructive conspiracy which from Pakistan to My Lai to the Pentagon Papers is showing its hand as the American way of death.

The peace of Christ, it goes without saying, is not won by such complicity. The way of peace is something else; necessarily a humiliated *via crucis* today – no less than in the year of our Lord. It requires that our lives lie open to the fiercest winds of change, that we confront together our fears, our despair and dread of life, that we resolve to renew ourselves each day in fraternities whose only charter is the gospel.

Merton said somewhere that if we perish, we will go down, not at the hands of madmen, but of cold war functionaries, certified sane, Eichmanns with fingers on the button. I am inclined to agree. I am inclined also to reflect on the perennial sanity commended by the gospel and Paul, the folly of the cross. Certainly we have had enough, until it sticks in the throat, of the sanity of powerful rakes whose progress is recorded in the Pentagon Papers.

What of this other sanity, verified in Christ, in the saints, verified once more in our lifetime? It intoxicates one to think of it – the continuity, the universalizing of conscience, the conduct of war resisters today. You must be as grateful as I am, seeing the Acts of our Good Years enacted again. Who would have dreamed a few staid years ago, that priests and nuns would be taken in the common dragnet, would refuse to betray others, would display an unnerving cool in the face of Big Huff and Puff?

The great return to roots has begun. You and I have seen only the beginning, only the first act. But even that beginning is enough to get the blood racing with exultation. Christians in America have struck free. We could once be counted on by Caesar – for the silence that kills, for bargains arrived at across the bodies of the victims, for a blessing on violence and a sanction on murder. No more of that.

We must be clearheaded about the price of sanity. I mean by 'the price' something quite concrete, as the authorities have already spelled it out to some of us. The price is refusal and resistance. If Caesar would make of the nation an abattoir, we refuse to be his executioners, his tourists, his do-gooders, his freeloaders. As Jesuits we will disrupt the business of death as usual; in our own communities we will perhaps eventually stop playing our nuanced dance of the mind, whose tune is beautiful and seductive, but for which someone must pay – inevitably someone other than ourselves. We will stop making liturgy an excuse for inaction, the life of the mind a cul-de-sac, our communities for cultural Brahmins.

Caesar is fed up with some of us; he is even, now and again, afraid of us. It is good that he should fear us: fear makes his hand unsteady. The fear that afflicts the great saves lives – at least some lives. And the saving of lives is, I take it, our business, even to the point of laying down our own.

I don't want to sound gnomic or occult here. If I have any regrets about the past years, they centre around the tardiness with which I went to Catonsville. If I had gone sooner, if I had had the gift of drawing other Jesuits with me, if a thousand Jesuits had come to their own Catonsville – and stood up to the law and the courts – what an effect we would have had, what horrors might have been averted!

But nothing of this happened. I was long bemused by a 'normalcy' that blinded my eyes. I had been equipped to deal only with normal times; beyond lay an abstract no man's, no god's land – a war like every previous war, a war my church approved, a war against which no sanction was involved, since it was an American war, and we were Americans.

The war was at worst a discomfiting episode. Normalcy was still possible; we would invoke normal good sense, expect it of our military and political leaders; bless those who were unlucky enough to be shipped off, regret the inevitable deaths. Who was to foresee that so small a cloud would shortly cover the sky, that a sinister and terrifying plague was even then incubating, that moral disaster, assassinations, large-scale murder of the innocent, deception in high places, idolatry of violence would become the simple order of the day?

The prison experience, a kind of harrowing of hell, also ploughs up one's own existence, his attitudes, his imagination, his use of language. His attitudes: Am I a believing man? His vocabulary: What words does a believer use in addressing his brothers from prison?

On the one hand, one is reluctant to use 'religious' terms; he grows sensitive to the bowdlerizing and bastardizing of religion in the service of oppression. We, too, have our chaplain, a captive of Caesar; more often than not, we have been judged, manacled, strip searched, our mail censored, our visits spied on – by religious men, good Germans 'doing their jobs,' good Catholics.

Yet I must also say something of the religious character of life here. Solitude, the presence of suffering, the breaking of men, the need and opportunity for prayer, these make one's faith more acute. I believe in Jesus Christ. He sustains my spirit, he speaks to me in my brothers and sisters. I reflect upon the hours when I lay close to death, and I confess my naïve surprise that I did not see

His face. I saw only the faces of Philip, of the doctor, of my fellow prisoners, sober with grief and shock. Were their faces the forms of His own? I do not doubt it.

There is another dialectic to things. Dying in prison, or living there, is from another point of view completely secular in character. Even at the point of death, I was not in any sense consoled, I had to struggle to remember that it was probably important to pray. It was as nearly impossible to pray as it was to breathe, a moving of mountains, a Sisyphus work of faith. God did not show his hand – or his face. Dying was a kind of banal continuum with living – crowded, messy, grey, noisy, a limbo by day or night. The senses are toned down, the body and mind tend to lassitude, the sweet stimulus and variety of the world are a forbidden fruit, a remembrance of aching grief. The outside world visits us, under strict supervision, as though we were terminal patients or mental defectives. The place is something like a Jansenist novitiate set up in opposition to the worst of all possible worlds – except that with us it is the world that must be protected against its own offscourings.

Too evil to be borne, or too virtuous to mix; in any case, locked up. It is the image of lockup (what stays in, what stays out) that strikes me as a way of expressing the secular 'taste' life carries here – unmistakable as brimstone on the tongue. We are locked up, a way of dramatizing the deep mystery of evil – are in purgatory for the accumulation of merit in Caesar's eyes, doing time in the pit, the languishing and labour that precede redemption. With this crucial difference – the human shape of God's love is absent, the search for ways of change, in life and society, the means to make us conscious, politically literate, alive to our world. No one in authority gives a literal damn; they are here to see that no inmate dare do so. The goodness implied in divine caring, responding to, prevenient to human goodness is excluded by law.

This means something quite simple and concrete, as far as prison discipline is concerned. Everything that touches on the life of prisoners must be literally second rate; as in hell. The quality of what is quaintly called 'custodial care' is second rate (though it absorbs some 95 per cent of the budget, a pretty exact application of national values, national military spending). Food, religion, books, programmes, edicts – all are dog-eared, outdated, tepid.

Nothing in prison corresponds to a deeply gravitational pull towards excellence that in the world outside, in the Society, existed at least at the edge of life, a gnawing in us, a call to us; the perfect sacramental mysteries, the homilies and texts, the demands made on our lives, prayer, chastity, the clear and consistent structure of a life the saints had lived, and we were invited to live. Nothing of this here; not even a show of some sort of desacralized humanism. We wear old army clothes, eat mediocre food with half an appetite, are cheated at the company store, defrauded in sweat shops putting together weaponry against Vietnamese. We listen to windjammers instructing us in law and order, are presumed to be as infantile and incoherent as our keepers, are ordered about in a cynical dumb show. The absence of ideas, alienation from nature, suppression of instinct, the presence of fear, the itch of violence – these are the ingredients of an ideological secularism, drawing on the dregs of bad religion, jingoism, despair of human nature.

Still we try to deal with this – because we believe, at the edge of unbelief. The absence of God is indeed a triumph of the state – but I reflect that, with a crude but altogether sound logic, Caesar may have created a situation in which faith comes into its own. He has nearly quenched the light. Does he serve to thrust us into the dark night, which is the proper atmosphere of faith? I believe the worst he can do is the prelude to the best which God will do. It may be that the lord of this world is already reduced to a slave's rule – dealing death to all that is parasitic and moribund in us. If we are hopeful, patient, modest, inventive, and firm of heart, we will see great things. Even we ...

Meantime, I suggest we take seriously a solemn warning set down some years ago by Philip and recently echoed by Gordon Zahn. The American church is in a worse moral position before history than was the German church under Hitler. For German Catholics, access to information on the Jewish question was extremely hard to come by; today, the truth about Vietnam is out. Then, protest was forbidden under the heaviest penalties; today penalties, even for conscientious lawbreakers, are comparatively slight.

In the baleful light of the deaths of whole peoples, deliberately and repeatedly inflicted, our neglect of the moral questions raised by wars, our petty concerns about religious renewal, seem to me a binding form of self-deception: good housekeeping in a plague-tormented city.

I must conclude that, for my part, to be a marginal Jesuit is a permanent state of life. I must draw from alienation the spiritual resources needed to persevere in my search for manhood, conscience, the will of Christ. Certainly I cannot be a Jesuit because I discover moral clairvoyance or heroism in its leadership. But my hope is strong that these qualities are emerging in a number of young Jesuits.

To all, the pledge I made a year ago still stands: I am at your side in the struggle; I ask you to stand at my side also.

Someday we will have our retreat together, and meditate and rejoice in our confessing brotherhood. Meantime, struggle. A world is possible in which the murder of children is not an acceptable 'way of life.'

My hand over the wall.

Daniel

Jim Forest · *Communities of Resistance*

Jim Forest, 'Communities of Resistance' and 'Developing the Alternative', *Seeds of Liberation* ed. Alistair Kee, SCM Press 1973, pp.32-35, 55-56, 59, 63-64, 67

It is the Catholic Worker I keep thinking of again and again, which has formed and birthed and delivered and pulled us forward again and again and again in the American Community. I have been thinking about that series of little places where people are welcomed without question and where the editors are perennially going to gaol, and where we see a great deal of death and of people dying in doorways, where we insist that there is some connection between the people who are dying in the doorways on our streets and the people who are dying in their houses in Indochina. Thinking of the Catholic Worker I think how very simple the whole thing is. How incredibly simple. None of us, for example, has to be an intellectual. I don't have to be an intellectual to respond, to see to keep the windows open, to be able to run out into the street. It's all in the gospels. Think of Chapter 25 of St Matthew's gospel: 'I was hungry and you fed me, I had no place to stay and you took me in. I was thirsty and you took care of my thirst. I was sick and you nursed me. I was in prison and you came to be with me.' These are the criteria of judgment, these are the criteria of *life* according to him, according to my brother Jesus, and it has marked all of us, Christian and non-Christian, in a very special way before and since. It's the very core of the whole Catholic Worker experience. We are involved in a premeditated attempt to be people of mercy and so a huge range of possibilities are opened up for us, as well as thousands closed. Obviously, for example, pacifism

has been absolutely inescapable to us; if we are going to talk about
feeding hungry people and being with hungry people, we are
certainly not going to be part of any process which creates hungry
people. We are certainly not going to be part of any process which
strips or burns the clothes or skins from people's backs. We are
certainly not going to be part of the process that creates the *need*
for hospitality of which war is the most glaring and ultimate
example. We are not going to be part of any of these things. These
possibilities are forever closed to us. We are not going to *create*
the need that we are called to respond to. We are simply going
to respond to that need – and thus, at the same moment, to ask
questions, not simply about how to respond today to this particular
person's problems, but to ask how it is that such a problem exists.
We see in that gospel an invitation to ask questions about suffering
and especially *unnecessary* suffering, which is what the term
'oppression' really means. How does it happen to be that Kitty
Genovese is knocked down and knifed dead, and how is it that no
one puts their life in the way of her death?

Inevitably as we explore the works of mercy in our day-to-day
contact with people who have been thrust out of society and left to
die on the streets, we come to make certain connections. It isn't
just our small block. We come to see that people are being thrust
out on the streets in huge numbers in other parts of the world –
and for essentially the same reasons. You know Daniel Berrigan
uses the phrase, 'dread of life'. We can speak of these things in
very economic and analytical terms, but it keeps coming back to
this deep fear of touching and of being touched, of actually having
a moment of hot contact with the reality of another's life; to *taste*
another's life, to overcome the fear of that, the fear of the stripping
that might happen if I discover that another person has needs. If
I really discover the need is there and feel that person's life has
been something like my own, I might have to give something up,
I might have to break the bread and pass it out instead of keeping
it for a hungry day.

Communion – community – communication. It is in the ironical
position of attempting to be in communion with people, to feel
their lives and urgencies and needs, that we discover the possibility
of giving. Giving is a way of life, it's not a voluntary thing, you
know. If you've looked out the window and you fail to respond,
you're dead. If you want to be alive, it's a necessity to respond.
So we look out that window and we see what is happening. We
break out of the place. And while responding we discover that,
while everybody has assured us that we were going to be dead out

there, that life on the other side of the window would be miserable and couldn't possibly be satisfied any more, that our basic needs couldn't be met in that kind of response, we discover instead that for the first time in our lives we are beginning to feel the meaning of the word 'happiness'. We are beginning to understand the gospels. We are beginning to understand why it is that Jesus begins the beatitudes – a meditation on happiness – with a few words on the subject of poverty and moves on. We begin to understand the ironic relationship between the willingness to risk and the possibility of feeling joy, of having joy. As Leon Bloy said, 'The most infallible sign of the presence of God is joy.' We discover for the first time that it is possible to be joyful, just when we are on the way – as others judge – to death. For the gospels are suddenly no longer insane. They make sense, and we discover there are absolutely no ways in which we can close ourselves off from suffering without ourselves being made dead. Such is the insight lived out daily at the Catholic Worker – and out of that, in Chicago and San Francisco and Milwaukee and all these different places has emerged much of what we know of now as The Resistance.

I think, too, of the example of David Miller whose wife and children are here in front of me, who was part of the Catholic Worker in 1965. It was he who lit our consciences on fire by taking his draft card and lighting it on fire in 1965. Do you recall the horror and astonishment of an amazing number of people about that? It surprised us more than any. *We* expected everybody to be too dead by then to notice a burning piece of paper. From that act right out of the Catholic Worker, a community of people emerged who began to see in the institution of conscription the kind of embodiment of our whole way of life; in every turn of life, not only in the military but in school and church, in business and subways, we realized we were objects to be subjected to conscription, to be told *how* to go, *where* to go, *what* to say, *what* to wear, how *not* to talk, what *not* to say, what to be in *dread* of, who to *work* for, *who to be willing to kill*. We saw in conscription what our whole society was about and it was symbolized by a draft card. We went on from there, with Philip Berrigan pouring blood with his friends in Baltimore, not on draft cards but draft records. We went on from there to see the records not just as objects to be stained but objects to be made useless. We began to re-cycle them. We found in these moments we were rediscovering the possibilities of worship, we were finally finding a current way of articulating the gospels and finally finding a way of worship. For while these actions were obviously political, they were even more deeply spiritual, religious, liturgical events. This was the way that we could celebrate and articulate the Mass, the Book, and it was inconceivable for us to speak of either Book or Bread as long as our contact with the draft was a contact of syllables thrown into the air and into other people's ears. It was only when we took this sacred property of the state, pieces of paper, and dared to suggest that this paper was responsible for death, and that this kind of property had no right to exist, that ears opened, that people in their anger, in their puzzlement became capable of wondering about conscience, wondering about life, wondering about the possibility of their lives not being subject to conscription wherever they happen to be.

There is a line in a poem of W. H. Auden's, who is a wonderful traditionalist but with the only kind of tradition worth having. He says, 'Prohibit sharply the rehearsed response.' In our experiments with resistance we were a scandal to pacifists as well as militarists in what we did – and in what we continue to do sometimes. It was not a rehearsed response. It was not something that Gandhi or Martin Luther King or Henry David Thoreau had done. It was even something that was a scandal to some of our friends within the Catholic Worker. Perhaps they thought that the subscription lists would get burnt by some counterpart of ours! A just worry. But we broke out of the rehearsed response in solidarity with a tradition which is only valuable because it is continually proposed that we do just that. The tradition is to invent. We did it in community; we did it with silence; we did it with bread and wine; we did it with Jews. We did it without any money, and we loved it. We were able to breathe, we were able to feel our hearts beating and the sound of ourselves again. We were able to embrace each other in a society that does not particularly like embracing – except vicariously in 'x' rated movies. We did not end the war but we began finding an element of the way out, a way of community, and of resistance and of invention that prays so to multiply that we will at last no longer need to kill, no longer need to keep blind. For all its failure, this was the only kind of success that we could see in our society; the only place where we saw the Bible and did not try to escape the room. It was the only way we could look at each other; the only we we could talk about love.

First of all, many of us have jobs. We tried to get away from this old movement clericalism where those very holy radicals had to pass the hat to people who were not so holy and say, 'Say, please give us some of your ill-gotten goods to keep us holy ones going.'

The term 'bread labour' has come up in the American movement. We really are trying to find ways of simply being examples of how anybody could step outside the consumer-addicting syndrome and live simply and do useful things that are important to other people and be sustained by that. I think we look back on a movement that is very much like the worst aspects of mediaeval Catholicism. 'We Monsignors and bishops and cardinals, and so forth, are to pass a collection basket all the time because "we have the truth and you guys don't, and we are sacrificing more".' You have to keep a very grim face for this process, because if you start getting happy and having fun, well this changes the whole reality of the situation, and people don't empty their wallets so quickly.

Sometimes they take the money. We do not consider that paying taxes. We consider that being robbed. But let me give you the example of a teacher at a little college in California. She put down on a US form that she had five or six dependants, which meant that she was not eligible to have taxes taken out due to the number of dependants she had. She claimed these dependants because she had five or six Vietnamese kids who were living there in a house that she had rented and they were completely economically dependent on her. They were in the US for major surgery, the rebuilding of melted faces, and shattered jaws and multiple breaks in the spinal column and things of that kind. They were her dependants even though the tax people are still threatening to send her to prison because they are not American citizens and she is not giving the money through a tax exempt foundation and she has no right to do those things except through the housebroken charities.

She is continuing to do that, and every once in a while the government grabs into her bank account and takes her car and sells it at an auction. But that is stealing, that's not paying taxes. We know that we get stolen from, we know that we cannot stop these robbers coming into the house, but we do invite them in and tell them to sit down and make themselves comfortable while we write out a cheque.

The whole business of taxes – I don't want to get hung up about that. I just offered it as a kind of symbol, or a sign or a ritual that it seems to me is connected to the business of trying to pronounce something on the state. I am simply intent not to condemn militarism and its domestic equivalent while I am meanwhile writing my cheque out; by subsidizing those things I feel that there would be some contradiction there and that people would have a right to be puzzled. Thus our communities have looked for ways somehow to resist taxes. There is not *a* way of resisting taxes but thousands of ways. There has recently been published a manual in the US of about one hundred and fifty pages of ways to resist taxes. There are some proposals on tactics, too; when the Internal Revenue Services have started seizing people's cars, friends have gone out and bought the cars and given them back. We have had instances when cars were bought for just fractions of a dollar because nobody else wanted to buy a car that was for sale for such reasons. These have become organized events. We have looked at taxes the way we have looked at draft. This is a way of discussing reality, and our response to this institution will make it possible for people (even if they continue paying taxes) to see their lives more imaginatively and to understand the ways in which they have been pushed about. They may not have noticed it, because it's been going on for so long and everybody else is being pushed about like that.

Now as far as the employment question is concerned, we have failed miserably in finding the kind of employment that is really appropriate, but we have been trying very hard. We think that society has a lot of surface needs that are not being met and that people would be happy to help support people who are meeting these needs. It has not been long since teachers were supported not by dollars but by gifts of food and bags of ground wheat to keep going, more a barter/subsistence thing. That is how it goes sometimes. I don't want to give you the impression we are some sort of angels that never get our nails dirty, that we always find ways of winning against Holy Mother the state, we don't, but we are fascinated with the idea of being more peaceful and we believe that we will only be a free and peaceful people when we ourselves as individuals are free and peaceful. It's going to come from both directions, but it's not going to come at all if it does not come out of our lives.

The only time in my life that I felt that I was really reading the gospels was in prison. The only people in my own society who have been able to make me feel that the Spirit is really breathing down our backs are people who have been in tremendous trouble. I don't mean just in the movement, but those people who are really trying to survive and be alive and to respond to life wherever they may be. It tends to be because they are people on the edge of death. They are people of the Bowery, East Harlem, etc., in tremendous jeopardy all the time. When they talk about anything it seems to me verified in a way that cannot possibly be when I am really speaking out of safety deposit vaults – which is, as you know, where the church has mainly been located these recent centuries. A fact we're trying to change.

Thomas Merton · *Contemplation in a World of Action*

Thomas Merton, *Contemplation in a World of Action*, Allen & Unwin, London and Doubleday, NY 1971, pp.157-65. © 1965, 1969, 1970, 1971 by the Trustees of the Merton Legacy Trust

This is not intended merely as another apologia for an official, institutional life of prayer. Nor is it supposed to score points in an outdated polemic. My purpose is rather to examine some basic questions of *meaning*. What does the contemplative life or the life of prayer, solitude, silence, meditation, mean to man in the atomic age? What can it mean? Has it lost all meaning whatever?

When I speak of the contemplative life I do not mean the institutional cloistered life, the organized life of prayer. This has special problems of its own. Many Catholics are now saying openly that the cloistered contemplative *institution* is indefensible, that it is an anchronism that has no point in the modern world. I am not arguing about this – I only remark in passing that I do not agree. Prescinding from any idea of an institution or even of a religious organization, I am talking about a special dimension of inner discipline and experience, a certain integrity and fullness of personal development, which are not compatible with a purely external, alienated, busy-busy existence. This does not mean that they are incompatible with action, with creative work, with dedicated love. On the contrary, these all go together. A certain depth of disciplined experience is a necessary ground for fruitful action. Without a more profound human understanding derived from exploration of the inner ground of human existence, love will tend to be superficial and deceptive. Traditionally, the ideas of prayer, meditation and contemplation have been associated with this deepening of one's personal life and this expansion of the capacity to understand and serve others.

Let us start from one admitted fact: if prayer, meditation and contemplation were once taken for granted as central realities in human life everywhere, they are so no longer. They are regarded, even by believers, as somehow marginal and secondary: what counts is getting things done. Prayer seems to be nothing but 'saying words,' and meditation is a mysterious process which is not understood: if it has some usefulness, that usefulness is felt to be completely remote from the life of ordinary men. As for contemplation: even in the so-called 'contemplative life' it is viewed with suspicion! If 'contemplatives' themselves are afraid of it, what will the ordinary lay person think? And, as a matter of fact, the word 'contemplation' has unfortunate resonances – the philosophic elitism of Plato and Plotinus.

It is a curious fact that in the traditional polemic between action and contemplation, modern apologists for the 'contemplative' life have tended to defend it on pragmatic grounds – in terms of action and efficacy. In other words, monks and nuns in cloisters are not 'useless,' because they are engaged in a very efficacious kind of spiritual activity. They are not idle, lazy, evasive: they are 'getting things done,' but in a mysterious and esoteric sort of way, an invisible, spiritual way, by means of their prayers. Instead of acting upon things and persons in the world, they act directly upon God by prayer. This is in fact a 'superior kind of activity,' a 'supreme efficacy,' but people do not see it. It has to be believed.

I am not interested, for the moment, in trying to prove anything by this argument. I am concerned only with its meaning to modern people. Obviously there are many who *believe* this in the sense that they accept it 'on faith' without quite seeing how it is possible. They accept it on authority without understanding it themselves, and without trying to understand it. The argument is not one which appeals to them. It arouses a curious malaise, but they do not know what to do about it. They put it away on a mental shelf with other things they have no time to examine.

The view of the contemplative life, which is quite legitimate as far as it goes, places a great deal of stress on the prayer of petition, on intercession, on vicarious sacrifice and suffering as work, as action, as 'something accomplished' in cloisters. And stress is laid on the idea that the prayers and sacrifices of contemplatives produce certain definite effects, albeit in a hidden manner. They 'produce grace' and they also in some way 'cause' divine interventions. Thus it happens that a considerable volume of letters arrives in the monastery or convent mailbag requesting prayers on the eve of a serious operation, on the occasion of a lawsuit, in personal and family problems, in sickness, in all kinds of trouble. Certainly, Catholics believe that God hears and answers prayers of petition.

But it is a distortion of the contemplative life to treat it as if the contemplative concentrated all his efforts on getting graces and favours from God for others and for himself . . .

The real point of the contemplative life has always been a deepening of faith and of the personal dimensions of liberty and apprehension to the point where our direct union with God is realized and 'experienced.' We awaken not only to a realization of the immensity and majesty of God 'out there' as King and Ruler of the universe (which He is) but also a more intimate and more wonderful perception of Him as directly and personally present in our own being. Yet this is not a pantheistic merger or confusion of our being with His. On the contrary, there is a distinct conflict in the realization that though in some sense He is more truly ourselves than we are, yet we are not identical with Him, and though He loves us better than we can love ourselves we are opposed to Him, and in opposing Him we oppose our own deepest selves. If we are involved only in our surface existence, in externals, and in the trivial concerns of our ego, we are untrue to Him and to ourselves. To reach a true awareness of Him as well as ourselves, we have to renounce our selfish and limited self and enter into a whole new kind of existence, discovering an inner centre of motivation and love which makes us see ourselves and everything else in an entirely new light. Call it faith, call it (at the more advanced stage) contemplative illumination, call it the sense of God or even mystical union: all these are different aspects and levels of the same kind of realization: the awakening to a new awareness of ourselves in Christ, created in Him, redeemed by Him, to be transformed and glorified in and with Him. In Blake's words, the 'doors of perception' are opened and all life takes on a completely new meaning: the real sense of our own existence, which is normally veiled and distorted by the routine distractions of an alienated life, is now revealed in a central intuition. What was lost and dispersed in the relative meaninglessness and triviality of purposeless behaviour (living like a machine, pushed around by impulsions and suggestions from others) is brought together in fully integrated conscious significance. This peculiar, brilliant focus is, according to Christian tradition, the work of Love and of the Holy Spirit. This 'loving knowledge' which sees everything transfigured 'in God,' coming from God and working for God's creative and redemptive love and tending to fulfilment in the glory of God, is a contemplative knowledge, a fruit of living and realizing faith, a gift of the Spirit.

The popularity of psychedelic drugs today certainly shows, if nothing else, that there is an appetite for this kind of knowledge and inner integration. The only trouble with drugs is that they superficially and transiently mimic the integration of love without producing it. (I will not discuss here the question whether they may accidentally help such integration, because I am not competent to do so.)

Though this inner 'vision' is a gift and is not directly produced by technique, still a certain discipline is necessary to prepare us for it. Meditation is one of the more important characteristic forms of this discipline. Prayer is another. Prayer in the context of this inner awareness of God's direct presence becomes not so much a matter of cause and effect, as a celebration of love. In the light of this celebration, what matters most is love itself, thankfulness, assent to the unbounded and overflowing goodness of love which comes from God and reveals Him in His world.

This inner awareness, this experience of love as an immediate and dynamic presence, tends to alter our perspective. We see the prayer of petition a little differently. Celebration and praise, loving attention to the presence of God, become more important than 'asking for' things and 'getting' things. This is because we realize that in Him and with Him all good is present to us and to mankind: if we seek first the Kingdom of Heaven, all the rest comes along with it. Hence we worry a great deal less about the details of our daily needs, and we trust God to take care of our problems even if we do not ask Him insistently at every minute to do so. The same applies to the problems of the world. But on the other hand, this inner awareness and openness makes us especially sensitive to urgent needs of the time, and grace can sometimes move us to pray for certain special needs. The contemplative life does not ignore the prayer of petition, but does not overemphasize it either. The contemplative prays for particular intentions when he is strongly and spontaneously inspired to do so, but does not make it his formal purpose to keep asking for this and that all day long ...

Real Christian living is stunted and frustrated if it remains content with the bare externals of worship, with 'saying prayers' and 'going to church,' with fulfilling one's external duties and merely being respectable. The real purpose of prayer (in the fully personal sense as well as in the Christian assembly) is the deepening of personal realization in love, the awareness of God (even if sometimes this awareness may amount to a negative factor, a seeming 'absence'). The real purpose of meditation – or at least that which recommends itself as most relevant for modern man – is the exploration and discovery of new dimensions in freedom, illumination and love, in deepening our awareness of our life in Christ.

What is the relation of this to action? Simply this. He who attempts to act and do things for others or for the world without deepening his own self-understanding, freedom, integrity and capacity to love, will not have anything to give others. He will communicate to them nothing but the contagion of his own obsessions, his aggressiveness, his ego-centred ambitions, his delusions about ends and means, his doctrinaire prejudices and ideas. There is nothing more tragic in the modern world than the misuse of power and action to which men are driven by their own Faustian misunderstandings and misapprehensions. We have more power at our disposal today than we have ever had, and yet we are more alienated and estranged from the inner ground of meaning and of love than we have ever been. The result of this is evident. We are living through the greatest crisis in the history of man; and this crisis is centred precisely in the country that has made a fetish out of action and has lost (or perhaps never had) the sense of contemplation. Far from being irrelevant, prayer, meditation and contemplation are of the utmost importance in America today. Unfortunately, it must be admitted that the official contemplative life as it is lived in our monasteries needs a great deal of rethinking, because it is still too closely identified with patterns of thought that were accepted five hundred years ago, but which are completely strange to modern man.

But prayer and meditation have an important part to play in opening up news ways and new horizons. If our prayer is the expression of a deep and grace-inspired desire for newness of life – and not the mere blind attachment to what has always been familiar and 'safe' – God will act in us and through us to renew the Church by preparing, in prayer, what we cannot yet imagine or understand. In this way our prayer and faith today will be oriented towards the future which we ourselves may never see fully realized on earth.